PRAISE FOR
HOW DO YOU MAKE THEM THIRSTY?

"Leadership aficionados in sports and in life will find many nuggets to grab ahold of in these pages, as Coach Phil Weber offers lessons and stories from working with some of the most elite talent and teams on the planet."

—**Bob Beaudine**, president and CEO, Eastman & Beaudine; *USA Today* best-selling author of *The Power of Who* and *2 Chairs*

"As a son, father, husband, CEO, and friend, the support and guidance I have received from others throughout my life has been a gift. I believe that part of developing ourselves is the process of developing others to the best of our abilities. As they learn, we learn. As they grow, we grow. When challenges arise, they're never dealt with alone. You'll benefit greatly from the wealth of knowledge Phil shares on mastering your reality … and then so will many others."

—**Isaac Lidsky**, *New York Times* best-selling author of *Eyes Wide Open: Overcoming Obstacles and Recognizing Opportunities in a World That Can't See Clearly*

"Phil has a great natural energy, passion, and curiosity in his blood. He has studied the process of player development as much as anyone I know. His book weaves all of that together with great examples and real stories that make this a fun, instructional, and fulfilling read."

—**Danny Ferry**, former NBA player and NBA front office executive

"I love this book because of Weber's focus and expertise on finding our own potential by enhancing that of others. In a world that thrives on competition and individual achievement, we measure potential and pursue success all wrong. By pursuing success in isolation—pushing others away as we push ourselves too hard—we are not just limiting our potential, we are becoming more stressed and disconnected than ever. Success and happiness are not competitive sports. Rather, they depend almost entirely on how well we connect with, relate to, and learn from each other."

—**Shawn Achor**, *New York Times* best-selling author of *The Happiness Advantage* and *Big Potential*

"Phil is a relentlessly positive leader. You will enjoy this fun ride and learn important strategies on how to get the most out of individuals and teams. This book is for empowering thoughts only!"

—**Erik Spoelstra**, Head Coach, Miami Heat

"When I was head coach for the Phoenix Suns, one of our rookies, Toby Bailey, told me he and some other players were doing a terrific summer workout program with a guy named Phil Weber. I had never heard of Phil, so I showed up to watch one of their sessions. It didn't take long for me to know that I needed what Phil had. That afternoon I offered him a job on my coaching staff with the Suns. His combination of infectious energy, sincere enthusiasm, and attention to detail was the best I'd seen up to that point and still is to this day. If you are someone who is responsible for helping other people develop, whether it is in basketball, work, or life, this book is a must-read. You will appreciate Phil's focus not just on skills, but also on the psychology of development and the importance of shaping an individual's mindset toward their growth. As far as what happened to Phil's career after that day—I'll let him tell you that story."

—**Danny Ainge**, President of Basketball Operations, Boston Celtics

HOW DO YOU MAKE THEM THIRSTY?

YOU CAN LEAD HORSES
(AND PEOPLE) TO WATER, BUT ...

HOW DO YOU MAKE THEM

THIRSTY?

A ROAD MAP FOR DEVELOPING
THE POTENTIAL IN OTHERS

PHIL WEBER

Advantage.

Published by Advantage, Charleston, South Carolina.
Member of Advantage Media Group.

ADVANTAGE is a registered trademark, and the Advantage colophon is a trademark of Advantage Media Group, Inc.

Printed in the United States of America.

10 9 8 7 6 5 4 3 2 1

ISBN: 978-1-64225-198-2
LCCN: 2020923402

Cover design by Carly Blake.
Layout design by Megan Elger.

This publication is designed to provide accurate and authoritative information in regard to the subject matter covered. It is sold with the understanding that the publisher is not engaged in rendering legal, accounting, or other professional services. If legal advice or other expert assistance is required, the services of a competent professional person should be sought.

Advantage Media Group is proud to be a part of the Tree Neutral® program. Tree Neutral offsets the number of trees consumed in the production and printing of this book by taking proactive steps such as planting trees in direct proportion to the number of trees used to print books. To learn more about Tree Neutral, please visit **www.treeneutral.com**.

Advantage Media Group is a publisher of business, self-improvement, and professional development books and online learning. We help entrepreneurs, business leaders, and professionals share their Stories, Passion, and Knowledge to help others Learn & Grow. Do you have a manuscript or book idea that you would like us to consider for publishing? Please visit **advantagefamily.com** or call **1.866.775.1696**.

To my parents, Nancy and Phil Weber: throughout my life you have continually blessed with me with so much love and support and have shown me by example what being a family is all about.

To Lila, my rock and best friend: it's so amazing going through this journey called life with you.

To my most precious daughter Soleil: your presence in my life, your continually infectious smile, and your generous heart make you the greatest thing that has ever happened to me.

I will love you for forever and a day.

CONTENTS

Dr. Micheal Clark

Phil Weber was ahead of his time. He helped NBA players increase their effectiveness by focusing not just on skills alone, but on their mindsets as well. He started using this approach before mindset really became a thing that so many sports teams and businesses now embrace as a competitive edge. I got to witness the results firsthand when Phil and I were on the staff of the Phoenix Suns together— he was an assistant coach, and I was the team physical therapist. I already knew Phil was a skilled, offense-minded coach. But what I also learned to appreciate about him was the way he helped players take the long view to develop beyond their playing skills. In particular, he has a way of helping the younger players understand that, to achieve and sustain success in the NBA, their mindset had to develop and mature along with their games.

Phil writes the same way he coaches—with high energy, passion, and a positive outlook on life. One of his guiding principles in this book is that all players are different. They all come from different backgrounds and have different life experiences. They learn differently, think differently, and respond to different rewards. What motivates one player might not make a bit of difference to another player, and you have to consider that when planning for their development. As a business owner and CEO, I can appreciate how that principle applies just as critically to developing people at work as well.

Whether you are a coach, teacher, parent, or business leader, chances are you have some responsibility for helping other people improve. We all need to know more about how to support others to become more effective at whatever their goals are. There is nobody better to learn it from than Phil Weber—a guy whom I saw help so many players, including MVPs, Hall of Famers, and many others, develop to their full potential.

Dr. Micheal Clark, DPT, MS, PT, CES, PES
Chairman, founder, and CEO, Fusionetics
Founder, National Academy of Sports Medicine
Advisory board: Under Armour, Hyperice,
NBA Strength and Conditioning Association, UNC, UGA

Mike D'Antoni

Phil Weber has an unusual story to tell about how he went from working out players for free in the summers to the bench of the coaching staff for the Phoenix Suns. His story shows exactly what he preaches: if you are willing to put yourself out there, stick with it, and keep a positive attitude, and if you're willing to learn, you can be successful.

I worked with Phil for ten straight years when we were on the coaching staff together with the Suns and then the Knicks. A big part of his work in developing players was to have them focus on the mental aspect of things, and he was a role model for that in a very genuine way. Nothing could get him down. He would keep moving forward with a positive attitude and never took things personally—even through setbacks, criticism, or other people rejecting his ideas. Phil's thing was staying on an even keel and being positive and helping people out as much as he could.

His upbeat attitude was infectious, and it carried over to the players and other coaches. It didn't matter whether we were in a slump or winning; he was the same genuinely positive guy. In particular, Phil had some great results developing our younger players. They appreciated having someone like him in their corner who really cared about them while pushing them to get better.

I'm glad Phil has taken the opportunity to write this book about developing others. In addition to some great stories from his time in coaching, he has a unique perspective when it comes to helping people get better both as players and as people. We can all learn from Phil's attitude: get up every day and attack it as a new day. As a society we have an obligation to see each day as a new opportunity to improve ourselves and to influence other people in a way that makes the world a little bit better. If we do that, as Phil says, "Good things will happen."

Mike D'Antoni

NBA Coach

Jim Caviezel

In some ways, Phil Weber's life and mine have paralleled. I met Phil at the UCLA Men's Gym in 1997 when I was on the brink of what would become the break of my career. In 1997 neither of us knew what was in store for us. Here I was, this unknown actor who still felt more like a basketball player, and Phil was working tirelessly toward his dream of being an NBA coach. Both of us had about a 1 percent chance of making that happen, and both of us believed we would. When I walked into that gym that day, Phil was working out pro athletes. He let me jump right in, and here I was, guarding Paul Pierce, who would be the tenth overall pick of the 1998 NBA draft. I was always a believer in the impossible. What was completely obvious from the first meeting with Phil was his commitment to making people better. That was the first day of our friendship. What struck me and stayed with me from that first day we met was that it didn't matter if I was a potential pro athlete or not.

Living in an environment where rejection and setbacks are just part of the landscape put me in the position to give up on many occasions. In order to survive in Hollywood, I had to restructure my thinking, formulate a plan, and work consistently to achieve the vision that I had for myself. That mindset drew me to Phil. Beyond his irreproachable work ethic, I saw someone who could communicate to me how to put my own strengths to use. That is truly priceless! The other bond we shared was a connection to Coach John Wooden. Coach Wooden was my father's basketball coach, and Coach would be indispensable in shaping Phil's own coaching philosophy. Phil spoke with awe about how Coach Wooden had taken the time to meet with him, an aspiring NBA coach, and validate his coaching vision. In like fashion, Phil took an interest in helping me be the best me that I could be even before anyone knew my name.

That is what makes Phil Weber special, and why this book, *How Do You Make Them Thirsty?*, will capture your attention as well. Your path, like mine, may not be a journey toward becoming a professional athlete, but you have some greatness in you. You have some gift that you were meant to share with the world. This book is many things. What it is not is *just* a sports book for aspiring athletes. It is a life manual on how, in practical ways, to go beyond your potential in whatever path inspires you. When I read this book, it did something for me that Phil does so effortlessly: it allowed me to look backward, to look forward, and mostly to focus on the moment that I am in with boundless gratitude. That is a Phil gift! "Focusing on the positive" may not be a Phil Weber original, but he has surely bought stock in that statement. In his professional and personal relationships, Phil not only lives by this motto, but exemplifies it. As he reminds us in his own words, "When you focus on the positives, it increases your resilience, and you realize that setbacks are surmountable and temporary." Which one of us cannot benefit greatly from such profound advice? Take my advice. This is a book worth reading!

With gratitude,
Jim Caviezel

INTRODUCTION

The beautiful thing about watching great basketball players is that they make the most difficult feats look easy. A Steve Nash no-look pass, a Kobe Bryant turnaround jump shot, a Joe Johnson floater, or an Amar'e Stoudemire spin-move dunk all look so simple on TV. But how did they develop those skills? Many people assume that it is simply a God-given talent—that these players won the genetics lottery by being born tall, strong, fast, and gifted.

Yet consider this. In 2019, there were 540,769 boys playing high school basketball. According to data from the NCAA, approximately 1 percent of those kids will play basketball at a Division 1 college. And getting to the NBA? The chances of one of those high school players making an NBA roster are less than 0.03 percent. *Elite* doesn't even describe the tiny sliver of the population you see playing in the NBA. The question is, How did they get there? A lot of those high school and college players are tall, strong, and fast. What differentiates the good from the elite?

What I have learned from the many NBA players and coaches I have had the good fortune to work with is the singular focus and dedication they have to getting better. What the casual observer can't know is what those players do behind the scenes, off camera, to improve themselves. There are countless hours of practice. Some of it is in organized team practices, but so much more of it comes as the result of individual players working out in airless gyms or cracked blacktop courts over the course of their young lifetimes. But it doesn't stop there. In my experience, it is a combination of dedication to the physical skills and a difference in mindset that distinguish the competent from the great. The truly great have a thirst that can be slaked only by their drive to improve.

> The truly great have a thirst that can be slaked only by their drive to improve.

Can you instill a thirst to learn? What can coaches, teachers, managers, parents, or anyone else responsible for the development of others do to help them become their best? It is my goal in this book to answer those questions in the best way that I know how. This book is not about me. It is about a framework for coaching, teaching, and learning about getting better. For much of what I discuss in this book, I was merely an observer. I'm simply addressing the subject through my personal experience working with some of the best players and coaches in the game of basketball. I have learned something from each and every one of them along my journey. And although I wrote this book from the perspective of basketball, it is about more than that. It is about life. My principles for developing other people—what I call *making them thirsty*—certainly evolved from my experience as a player in college and as a coach in college and the NBA. But they are also heavily influenced by the interactions I have had with business leaders, the many books I have read, the interviews with experts that I have studied and deconstructed, and my own personal struggles and accomplishments. I have no idea how my life would have turned out had I not been so fortunate to learn from so many teachers, whether or not they were aware that they were teaching me something. I will be forever grateful for all the lessons I learned along my journey.

I have always seen my car as my classroom and have viewed my twenty- to thirty-minute commutes over the years as a perfect time to grow. Reading widely and listening have done many things for me. The first is that they taught me that a true principle is timeless. I have seen may examples of this, including Roman emperor Marcus Aurelius. Not only is he considered one of the great leaders of all time but also he was equally revered as a Stoic philosopher. Even though he died more than eighteen hundred years ago, the principles he describes in his book *Meditations* are as relevant today as they were during his lifetime. A more recent example is Napoleon Hill. He wrote his classic book *Think and Grow Rich* over eighty years ago, and many leaders swear by the effect it has had on their lives. The book has had a rebirth in popularity among twenty- and thirtysomething entrepreneurs, and its lessons are just as applicable today.

The second thing that reading outside of my professional field has done is to show me that true principles are not specific to any one industry. True principles transcend any sport, hobby, or vocation. People are people, so it doesn't matter what sport you play or what business you're in. True, valued principles will govern regardless. The main life principles such as honesty, humility, hard work, loyalty, persistence, and love are essential, no matter what you do.

All of us have some degree of responsibility for helping other people develop, whether that is in our role as parent, partner, manager, mentor, or coach. In this book, I address a lot of the how-to that should be helpful to any reader. But I go beyond that to explore the why-to as well, because if we have clarity on the *why*, the *how* is clearer. Understanding the why also represents a mindset change for most of us, as it is so easy to focus on the mechanics and task aspects of the developmental relationship we have with others. In my experience, the biggest opportunity to have influence as a coach did not occur when I was sitting on the team bench during an NBA game. Rather, it was from the individual work I did with hundreds of college and professional players (in one-on-one workouts during the team's season or during summer workouts) to address specific aspects of their games. To be helpful to them, I had to understand their *why* before I could help them with the *how*.

There is no single best way to develop basketball players. In fact, a coach should always strive to continue to grow and understand new ways to relate information and instill quality habits. All players are unique. A method of teaching or motivating one player may fall on deaf ears for another. I have seen coaches who are brilliant tacticians fail because they use a one-size-fits-all mindset toward relating to players.

The secret is to have a planned approach but to be willing to flex based on the needs and learning styles of the players. For example, Jalen Rose was a smooth, smart player for the Indiana Pacers. Jalen and I worked together for three consecutive off-seasons in my group workouts at the old Men's Gym at UCLA. After those group sessions, Jalen and I would work to improve his shot. As we did so, we recognized that his shooting issue was mostly about wrist placement. Through repetition and the use of a specific technique that involved a weighted ball, Jalen was able to improve his shot. Because of his willingness to work hard and his unique learning style, he required very few verbal cues. He listened to our initial instructions, then diligently practiced his technique. Jalen was a hard worker by nature and became the informal leader of those off-season workouts. His intensity always raised the level of our group sessions, which was awesome to see. His hard work paid off when he was recognized as the Most Improved Player after the 1999–2000 season.

While on the coaching staff of the New York Knicks, I had the opportunity to work with forward David Lee. He is another example of a motivated, hardworking player—but with a different learning style. We worked with David to correct a similar shooting issue based on wrist placement. Unlike Jalen, David's learning style was more about creating a mental checklist to correct his shot. He abbreviated this checklist to a verbal mantra he recited to ensure that he was following the right mechanics when he went up for a shot. Fellow assistant coach Dan D'Antoni also helped shape David's mindset in order to strengthen his confidence. Two players, a similar issue, but entirely different developmental solutions.

My approach has worked for me, and I think it can be helpful to you. I start with a plan constructed with building blocks that are clear and thorough, then I pay attention to the unique learning and developmental needs of each player along the way, making shifts to accommodate their individual needs. After that it is up to the players to put in the work. By doing so, we get these players to where they want to be with better and faster results. I have laid out these building blocks as chapters in this book and have organized them into four sections: the context, the relationship, the plan, and the process. It is my goal to lead you through this step-by-step approach to helping another person excel in their developmental journey. Let's get them thirsty!

SECTION 1:
THE CONTEXT

THE ROAD

As I drive along my dreams appear
    my hands let go, my heart will steer

A vision of success is the driving force
    that inspires me through life's treacherous course

Success is like a journey that knows no end
    an unquenchable thirst I treat as a friend

As long as I breathe I'll push to do more
    but in this game we call life it's hard to keep score

For all men are different with their own dreams and goals
    One man's Chevy is another man's Rolls

A passion in life to fill a vital need
    is the common trait in all that eventually succeed

The concept of failure I don't understand
    I will constantly move forward and on my feet I will land

I see what's before me, each day I will try
    with my feet on the ground, to reach for the sky

—Phil Weber

CHAPTER 1

THIS IS GOOD, BUT WHY?

In this business, if you lose, you're gonna get fired. If you win, you still may get fired. That's the hard part.

—Stan Van Gundy

"Phil, we are going in a different direction."

That's sports speak for "you're fired." This, after ten years of working my way up as an assistant college coach, first at the University of Florida, later at Chaminade University, and now at Iona College. In my mind, nobody worked harder than I did. At Iona, I was the first person to arrive for work at the Mulcahy Center every morning and usually the last to leave. In my plan, I was on a trajectory to be a college head coach. Instead, I was suddenly out of basketball.

FOCUS ON THE POSITIVE

This is good, but why? It's easy for me to look back and realize that getting fired was a gift. If that had never happened, I wouldn't be in the NBA right now. (More on that shortly.) The challenge is to keep a positive perspective in the moment when something bad is happening to you. As James Allen said in *As a Man Thinketh*, circumstances do not make a man; they define him to himself.[1] For me, every end of the season became job application time. I was always looking to grow and to climb up the coaching ladder. I applied for every open job that would better my situation. I got rejection letter after rejection letter, and the stack of papers grew quite high. With every single letter I received, I would always greet it with the same thought: *This is good, but why?* Sometimes the reasons were a stretch: *It's good that I didn't get this job in Idaho because it would take me away from my family in New York.* This way of thinking allowed me to focus my brain on the positive. I'm not talking about sour grapes; I'm talking about being able to see the positive in everything we look at. I don't mean to say that it is easy, but it changes your outlook and increases your resilience. And once you have instilled that resilience, your brain is hardwired to look at all setbacks as surmountable and temporary. They simply become part of your unique journey.

Many recent studies show that people who express gratitude are in general happier, healthier, and easier to be around.[2] I didn't know that back in 1995, but I sent a follow-up thank-you letter after every one of those rejections. Again, we can train our brains to focus on the

---

1   James Allen, *As a Man Thinketh* (New York: St. Martin's Essentials, 2017).

2   Amy Morin, "7 Scientifically Proven Benefits of Gratitude That Will Motivate You to Give Thanks Year-Round," *Forbes*, November 23, 2014, https://www. forbes.com/sites/amymorin/2014/11/23/7-scientifically-proven-benefits-of-gratitude-that-will-motivate-you-to-give-thanks-year-round/#2a718160183c.

positive while still dealing with the reality of any situation. The other thing that I did was to depend on the relationships I had in my life to try to discover what else might be possible for me.

BE READY FOR OPPORTUNITY

One of my best friends in the world was a guy named Bret Bearup. We met in high school and played together on All-Star teams that traveled to Europe and Canada. I

> We can train our brains to focus on the positive while still dealing with the reality of any situation.

had a key to my elementary school gym, and Bear and I would work on our games together. Bear went on to play at Kentucky and then finished law school there as well. Afterward, he immediately started an investment firm that specialized in professional athletes and entertainers. The rules determined that sports agents could not sponsor trips for amateur basketball players, but Bear found a loophole in the NCAA bylaws and determined that financial companies could. When I was at Iona, every year Bear would call and ask me to come work for him. Every year I would say, "Hey, leave me alone, Bear. I'm coaching!"

But now I was out of coaching and getting one rejection letter after the other, and I was barely making rent payments. Bear kept persisting, so I went down to see him in Lexington. He met me in front of his beautiful building, and we took the elevator up to his office. It was a glass elevator, and as we watched the Lexington skyline sink below us, he asked, "When we were traveling around as high school players on those teams, did you ever think I would be someone who could own a building like this, Phil?"

I had an immediate paradigm shift, and I went to work with Bear. I learned the basics of the business, passed some licensing requirements, and dived in. The crazy thing is, I had just made the move to leave coaching, and the first thing Bear told me was that we were going to take a team of high school All-Americans to Europe and that I was going to coach the team. These were highly sought-after players from all across the country. The teams were always comprised of sophomores and juniors. The first team we took over was super talented and included Baron Davis, Ricky Davis, Jason Kapono, and Dean Oliver, all future NBA players. Bear understood the way I could relate to and get along well with young players. He also knew I had a knack for helping players get better.

After agreeing to join Bear, I decided to live in Los Angeles. Bear did not have a presence on the West Coast, and I could do this job from anywhere. I had some friends in LA, and I figured there was a lot to do there—two NBA teams, two NFL teams (at the time), two baseball teams, Hollywood, great weather—so why not go? I moved to California, and that's when my life changed in a way I could have never imagined.

CHAPTER 2

WORK YOUR WAY TO LUCK

Your purpose in life is to find your purpose
and give your whole heart and soul to it.

—Buddha

After I moved to California, I reconnected with Baron Davis, who was from LA. I told Baron that we should get together because I believed I could help him. Baron was interested, and he agreed. I told him that I didn't know my way around LA at all, so Baron suggested that we meet at the old Men's Gym at the UCLA campus.

THE LEAST GLAMOROUS JOB IN BASKETBALL

There was no Hollywood glitz surrounding the Men's Gym. It was old (built in 1932), boxy, and stuffy. An article in *Sports Illustrated* referred to it as the "BO Barn" for its hot, airless atmosphere. What it lacked in glitz it made up for in history.[3] This was the home of one of my heroes, UCLA's former head coach John Wooden, prior to the construction of Pauley Pavilion in 1965.

On a September day in 1995, Baron and I walked into the building, past the ROTC offices and up the cement stairs, and pulled open the door to the gym. I was amazed to see thirty NBA guys out on the court, and I remember thinking, *Are you kidding me? This is absolutely crazy! What is this?* I had no idea that this was where many NBA players worked out against each other during the off-season. After those players finished their session, Baron and I hit the court, and that was the beginning of an informal summer workout program that led me to work and build relationships with over one hundred NBA players.

I worked all day in that old gym, sweeping the floor in between sessions and giving it everything I had. I never charged those players anything, but I was learning so much from each of them and developing strong relationships with guys like Jalen Rose, Paul Pierce, Chauncey Billups, Ty Lue, and many others whom I worked with over the next three and a half summers. Most importantly, I was learning how to focus my skills on helping players get better. Eventually I had four major NBA agents reaching out to me to get their guys ready for the NBA draft workouts. I learned that every summer there was a scheduled time for the NBA guys to play their pickup games in the Men's Gym. I would work my guys out before they started their games. I had to grab whatever time I could; sometimes that meant an early start or a late-night finish.

---

3   Alexander Wolff, "The Coach and His Champion," *Sports Illustrated*, April 3, 1989, https://vault.si.com/vault/1989/04/03/the-coach-and-his-champion-john-wooden-had-53-loving-years-with-his-wife-nell-now-shes-gone-and-he-struggles-alone.

By the third summer, I had worked with many NBA guys in that old gym. One of those players was Toby Bailey, a former UCLA star who was drafted by the Phoenix Suns. In the spring, after the NBA season of 1999, Toby kept telling me that Danny Ainge, the head coach of the Suns, wanted to come watch me work him out. I thought, *That's fine. He can watch the workout. He'll tell me what to do with Toby. He's the NBA guy, right? I'll do whatever he wants me to do—footwork, dribble moves, whatever he has in mind for Toby.*

ONE PERSON CAN CHANGE YOUR LIFE

One day after my conversation with Toby, I was coaching a team in the LA summer pro league for a friend of mine who was an agent for European players. It was an early game, and it felt to me like the JV game just before the varsity game. As my game ended, I saw Danny Ainge waiting for the NBA players' game that would start next. I had never met Danny, but I knew who he was. I walked over and introduced myself. "Hey, Danny, I'm Phil Weber."

Danny paused as he put my face with my name and said, "Oh, Phil."

I told him, "I'm working Toby and some other guys out tomorrow, and you're welcome to come watch. We're starting at eight in the morning."

The next day Danny showed up for that fateful workout that included Toby, Darrick Martin, and Mitchell Butler. The session lasted for about an hour and a half. After we finished, Danny walked up to me and asked, "Phil, can I talk to you?" Of course I said yes, and then he asked, "What's your background?" I thought to myself, *That's an odd question.* I told him that I was a former college coach now working with a bunch of NBA guys. I will never, for the rest of my life, forget what Danny Ainge told me next. He said that he's been playing basketball his entire life, and he's been in the NBA for the last fourteen years as a player and three as a coach, and a perfect workout was something that existed only in his mind until that day. As gracious a compliment as that was to hear from Danny, it is what he said to me next that has reverberated through my mind for the last twenty years and changed the course of my life. "Phil, what would it take in compensation to get you on my coaching staff?"

We sat down and started talking. I didn't jump at it because I had some other things brewing, and I wanted to be up front with Danny. I told him that I was developing an academy with Kiki VanDeWeghe that was scheduled to start in August. I also told him that I had a friend who was buying an NBA team and that there was some potential to work with him. (That friend was Stan Kroenke, but I didn't mention his name out of confidentiality.) Danny said, "Well, I'll give you a ten-month contract." Then I thought to myself, *Whoa, this is good.*

And with that, I went from being completely out of coaching to the bench in the NBA. Although I am writing this from the perspective of the effect that it had on me, what shouldn't get lost in this story is that Danny Ainge was a visionary and a pioneer in the area of player development. Today it seems like every NBA has eight player development guys. But Danny was the first NBA coach I knew of who hired someone specifically for that role. I'm convinced that anyone working in the NBA right now has one person they can point to who gave them

> I'm convinced that anyone working in the NBA right now has one person they can point to who gave them their break.

their break. I will forever be indebted to Danny Ainge. Danny has always been an innovator and a creative leader, whether he was playing or coaching or now in his current job as executive director for the Boston Celtics. It was his forward-thinking approach to player development, combined with the work I had done up to that point to put me in a position to cross his path, that converged in that old gym. I've been in the NBA ever since.

SECTION 2:
THE RELATIONSHIP

RIVER OF LIFE

Our lives are like rivers flowing from dusk to dawn,
But what will they say when I am gone?
Those who say they don't care, I'll tell you they do,
A lesson in life I've learned to be true.

We all go through life confused and unsure …
Did I constantly persist and fight to endure?
Was I a man of honesty, selflessness, and pride,
Or did my integrity vanish like the changing tide?
Did I cherish my woman with all my soul? To share life's beauty was
my ultimate goal.
When you think of my life, examine a theme: Did I fight through
hardship and stay true to my dream?

The Lord will measure my life and my deeds.
Did I care for others and look out for their needs?
Did I live for each day and treat time as a friend?
For my days are now over, all good things must end …
Like a river your dusks will flow to dawn; please take care, now that
I am gone.

—Phil Weber

CHAPTER 3

BUILD TRUST AND RESPECT

If you have some respect for people as they are, you can be more effective in helping them to become better than they are.

—John W. Gardner

The previous two chapters provided some context for my journey and how my career focus evolved to player development. The rest of the book is more of the how-to. Although my experience has been specifically with basketball players and coaches, much of what I have learned applies to anyone who is helping other people get better at something, such as leaders, parents, teachers, and others.

There is absolutely nothing more important in the process of helping another human being in their developmental journey than establishing a strong, positive relationship. The cornerstone of the relationship must be built on mutual trust and respect.

HONOR THE MUTUAL COMMITMENT

I never take it for granted that when I work with a player to help improve some aspect of their fundamentals, they are, to some extent, putting themselves in my hands. For me, it is both a humbling and an exhilarating process. That was definitely the case when I was on the coaching staff with the Phoenix Suns and I got the opportunity to work with Boris Diaw. My initial experience with Boris was all about trust.

We acquired Boris from the Atlanta Hawks in the Joe Johnson trade in the summer of 2005. Boris, a former professional player in France, was supremely talented, deceptively athletic, and one of the smartest players I have ever coached. When he joined the Suns, it was widely accepted that to really contribute, he would need to shoot the ball better.

In the process of gaining Boris's trust, a few things happened to help that along. An urgency and bigger opportunity emerged when Amar'e Stoudemire had a season-ending surgery. Alvin Gentry, who was a fellow assistant coach and highly respected for his experience, mentioned to Boris, "You saw what happened to the last guy that Coach Weber worked with. I'd trust him." He was referring to Joe Johnson, who just received a $75 million contract in the trade.

Boris was supremely intelligent, and I knew that he would be analyzing my every move. I felt that I really needed to get his attention and to show him how much I believed in his talents and potential. At the beginning of our first workout, I told him, "Boris, if you trust me, not only will you and your family benefit, but so will generations of Diaws." That is something I had never said before and have never said again, but my gut told me it was something that would help to start the process and establish a connection with Boris.

We got to work. Boris was intensely focused during every workout every single day. He listened intently, but he was always a player who would challenge you on why you were doing something. Early in the process, I mentioned that it would take him six weeks for the things we were working on to become closer to automatic. Boris made great strides, but right around the seven-week mark, he said in his French accent, "Phil, it's past six weeks, and I don't feel I'm automatic."

Boris's personal development was critical for our team that year. Three important factors led to Boris's success. First was the opportunity to play for a great coach, future Hall of Famer Mike D'Antoni. Second was playing on a Suns team loaded with talent led by Hall of Fame point guard Steve Nash. Third, and probably the biggest factor, was Boris's daily dedication and hard work that positioned him to win the NBA's Most Improved Player Award. I'm not sure where Boris is at this moment, but due to his success, he doesn't need to work, and he could very well be traveling the world in his yacht.

Any player—or any student, child, or coworker—will know right away if you are sincere about helping them. They will quickly decide if you really care about their development or if you are just punching a time card and going through the motions. The player will continually be evaluating your interest in the teaching and learning process. As Theodore Roosevelt said, "Nobody cares how much you know until they know how much you care." Over time the deeper levels of the relationship will grow as the player learns that they can trust you and that you have their (and not your own) best interests in mind. How do you build trust and respect? It's a combination of displaying personal integrity and doing it consistently over time.

A great example of how a coach cares about their players is Tim Grgurich. Grg, as he is endearingly called, is one of the most respected assistant coaches ever. He embodies every positive trait that a coach can have. He is energetic, knowledgeable, giving, humble, and passionate about the profession. Most importantly, every single player he's worked with feels how much he cares about them and their improvement, and that is the cornerstone of the foundation Grg builds with players. Years ago, Grg started an August camp for players with a couple of coaches, and it has grown to be *the* NBA event in August. It is my opinion that one day he will be in the Hall of Fame because of all that he's giving to the game of basketball.

I have worked with several coaches who are able to show players their commitment and care, and they have all influenced my approach to establishing a strong player relationship. The following five actions are not an exhaustive list of the ways to build trust and respect, but in my work, I try to pay particular attention to each of them.

BE PREPARED

Preparation is everything. To me, being prepared means that I have a plan. I never wing it. The players I work with have busy schedules. They depend on me to make efficient use of their time, and that happens long before we walk onto the court together. I have to be intense in my approach and plan the workout specifically for that player, for that day. When you bring that level of preparation, you demonstrate that you care enough about the relationship (not just the task) to make the most of their investment in time and focus.

What the casual basketball fan might not understand is that an NBA team is a complex system of many people and hundreds of moving parts. All this has to come together within the context of a team. It is all about the team, and I have been lucky to work with some teams that had exceptionally strong cultures. Some of you are in industries that have nothing to do with sports, but the same thing applies to the business world. Steve Jobs said, "Great things in business are never done by one person. They're done by a team of people." You are part of a team that does most of its work away from the customer. There is probably no way that I can understand what goes into your product behind the scenes.

There are a lot of elements to team culture, and preparation level is one of the most critical. Every NBA coaching staff I have been a part of made a point to meet and discuss what we wanted to accomplish in practice. Being successful in the NBA and being prepared are synonymous. All the coaches I worked with met approximately two hours before every practice. When I was an assistant coach with the Phoenix Suns and we had an away game, head coach Scott Skiles

> There are a lot of elements to team culture, and preparation level is one of the most critical.

met with the coaching staff every day at breakfast to prepare. Bonus benefit—Scott always picked up the tab, so it saved on my per diem! Over the ten years that I worked under head coach Mike D'Antoni, when we were on the road, he always set a meeting time that started two hours before the team bus left. If we were at home, our planning meeting would be two hours before practice started. It was always two hours before, no matter what. None of us ever had to ask him if we were going to have a meeting or what time it started. It was set in stone. I had a personal standard that I kept. I would prepare at least ninety minutes before every coaches' meeting on the road. If it was a home game, my prep was a couple of hours every morning.

I learned firsthand why there was an NBA saying that coaches sleep in the summer. That level of preparation allowed me to take a deeper dive into my own preparation for that particular meeting. In the Suns arena, there is a ramp leading in from the street, and that is where front office staff, coaches, and players park. The lowest space closest to the arena entrance is reserved for the owner, the next one is for the GM, and the one next to that is for the head coach. After that third space, it's open parking the rest of the way up the ramp. I made it my habit, for my nine years with the Phoenix Suns, to be the first one in every day, so that fourth space was invariably mine. I never forgot how lucky I was to have that job, and I wanted to work as hard as I could to be as prepared as possible.

Does that sound like too much preparation? It wasn't. Be prepared. It goes a long way in showing—not just telling—the other person that they can trust you to be ready.

BE PRESENT

In the past, whenever I heard someone talk about being present, it struck me as some vague new age jargon. I didn't fully grasp the concept. It has since become something that I pay close attention to. What does being present look like in action? For me, it is a heightened awareness. It means that I am paying attention to what is going on around me, and I am doing my best to make the other person know that they are the most important thing in my life at that moment. I am paying attention to them. I am 100 percent in the moment with them. I pay attention to how they are responding to the way I am teaching them. Is it working for them? If not, why not? Can we both get lost in the teaching and learning together?

If you are a manager and one of your employees is in your office sitting in the chair across from you, they are likely there for an important reason. At least, it is important to them. Do you have a white-knuckle grip on the arms of your chair? Are you glancing at your cell phone while they talk? Are you interrupting them? Is there a loop playing in your head that says, *How can I end this meeting? How can I end this meeting? How can I end this meeting?* Guess what? The other person will notice every one of those cues. When they leave your office, they will feel even worse. Not only is their issue still unresolved but also they didn't feel listened to.

Being present is also about truly listening, not only with your ears but also with your eyes. Are you fully listening to what the person is saying, or are you thinking about what you are going to say next? Business author Stephen Covey calls that situation *dueling monologues*. He explains that listening to someone fully is like giving them psychological air. They don't notice they have it. If you don't listen and they don't feel affirmed, they realize they don't have it. Like air, it becomes all they want.

BE CONFIDENT

Be clear with yourself about what you bring to the table. Phil Jackson, one of the winningest coaches in NBA history, said, "I think the most important thing about coaching is that you have to have a sense of confidence about what you're doing. You have to be a salesman, and you have to get your players, particularly your leaders, to believe in what you're trying to accomplish on the basketball floor."[4] When working with NBA players like Boris Diaw or Amar'e Stoudemire to improve their skills, it could be easy to be in awe of the players'

---

4   NBA, *The NBA at 50* (New York: Random House, 2003).

presence. However, I am fully aware of what I am bringing to the session. Just like these players, I worked my tail off to get to this stage; I just followed a different journey.

Many people deal with a strong negative force that the management literature calls the *imposter syndrome*. People who suffer from it are constantly anxious about being found out for what they really are. At least, that's how they think. You can imagine how that would show up if you felt that way. That has never been a problem for me. Not because I have a huge ego but because I have put in the time, and I know it. In his book *Outliers*, Malcolm Gladwell talks about the ten-thousand-hour rule, in which he credits the mastery of a skill to extreme practice, as opposed to smarts or other inherited characteristics.[5] In my case, I credit my years of focused experience working one-on-one with basketball players. I was working out basketball players in gyms from sunup to sundown years before I ever became an NBA coach. I have a relationship of mutual trust and respect with the players that is hard for me to define but that is the combined result of our journeys coming together on the court for a workout. We don't discuss it because we don't have to. It's more of an unspoken mutual respect.

In the process of building trust and respect, I believe that my hard work and focus will be apparent to the players I work with. Have you thought about that for yourself? My guess is that if you spent some time honestly considering your background and experience, you would have a clearer, more confident picture of your role. If you have made the decision to continually grow and improve in your approach, I'm sure you will take this to heart.

---

5   Malcom Gladwell, *Outliers: The Story of Success* (New York: Little, Brown, 2008).

BE ENERGETIC

"Phil Weber!" That's how I answer my phone. I know one thing for certain: I control my state of being 100 percent of the time. I bring energy and enthusiasm to everything I do because it is a choice. I'm guessing that some of the people who know me dial my number, then hold the phone out at arm's length until I answer. Granted, some of that is probably genetic, as I have always been a natural extravert. But at some point, I decided that I was going to meet my life with enthusiasm. I'm not talking about being over the top, in your face, or overbearing. I'm talking about my personal leadership presence and a standard that I set for myself. It is my goal to bring a boost to whatever time you and I spend together. The same goes for walking into a group and adding positive energy whenever I can.

This is a critical factor in the work that I do to help players develop. Some days players just don't feel like working out. Sometimes they're recovering from an injury. Other times it might be an early workout on a cold, rainy morning. And because they are all human, some days they just might not feel up to it. (Except Kobe Bryant, but more on that later.) When that happens, I want them to know that they can depend on me to bring energy and a spark to the work we do together.

This also carries over when I speak with business audiences and executive groups. Nobody wants to sit and listen to someone drone on. I try to connect with audiences by telling compelling stories in an energetic way. But most importantly, I try to help them see the application of the lesson in their world. Even though those interactions can be relatively short, there is still a relationship involved between the audience and me, and these principles about respect and trust play out there as well.

BE RELIABLE

In its simplest form, this one is easy to understand. Do what you say you are going to do. Make sure that your actions follow your words. It is the easiest way to build up your level of integrity. Period.

> Do what you say you are going to do. Make sure that your actions follow your words.

There's one study from the business world that sticks in my mind. Years ago, researchers at the Center for Creative Leadership were curious about why there were some executives who, after having built an impressive track record of success over the course of their careers, eventually derailed. They were fired, demoted, or passed over for promotion. The research showed that all the executives they studied (both successful and derailed) made mistakes in their careers—some small, some large.[6] Most of the time, these executives learned a lesson, worked harder, and came back from it. But there was one kind of mistake that the researchers labeled as "management's only unforgivable sin," and that was betraying a trust. When they looked deeper, it simply meant that the subjects in the study derailed because they didn't do what they told other people they were going to do.

It sounds simple, but it isn't. Most people think about this as failing to follow up, and don't get me wrong, that's a big part of it. The other part might be caused by taking on too much or not delegating some of your workload. Do what you say you are going to do. Why is not doing so an unforgivable sin? Because once you burn someone, it will always be in the back of their mind and they will question whether they can depend on you.

---

6   Morgan W. McCall Jr., Michael M. Lombardo, and Ann M. Morrison, *The Lessons of Experience: How Successful Executives Develop on the Job* (New York: Free Press, 1988).

If you want to build something solid that will endure over time, lay a strong foundation. When it comes to relationships, that foundation is mutual trust and respect.

CHAPTER 4

BE THE EXAMPLE

Be the change you wish to see in the world.

—Mahatma Gandhi

Establishing the trust and respect we discussed in chapter 3 is just the beginning. You don't check it off your list and move on. It is an ongoing effort that requires feeding and watering. I have always tried to do this by presenting myself in a professional and focused way— by setting the example. Otherwise, how can I expect the players I work with to do the same thing?

EARLY EXAMPLES HAVE BIG IMPACT

My parents never lectured me about the importance of hard work, and I don't remember them ever talking about it. I do remember very clearly seeing them model hard work every single day. It was who they were, part of their DNA. My dad was a full-time teacher and coach. To ensure that our family never wanted for anything, he built a successful business from scratch, providing services to commercial real estate owners. My father started by pushing a hand sweeper in a parking lot at 5:00 a.m. before he taught a full day of high school physical education, followed by coaching after school. Because of his personality and determination, he expanded to working with different commercial real estate companies and built the business over time. The business grew to provide any service that large office parks or shopping centers needed for their parking areas, such as paving, painting, landscaping, and snow removal. Dad ran the business, and my mother ran the office, took customer calls, and kept the books, all the while managing the chauffeuring and family issues. They are a great team. They both worked their tails off, and as a kid, I jumped right in to help. That's what our family did. One summer I put down every striped line and handicapped parking stall in the Smith Haven Mall parking lot on Long Island. I called myself the greatest shopping center artist alive because 99.9 percent of the lines were straight. I'd have to get up at two in the morning because you can't paint when cars are there. I'd load the paint, put my running shoes on, and head out. My attitude was, "Let's go!"

SHOW, DON'T TELL

My parents never had to tell me about the importance of working hard because they modeled it. My dad is such a nice guy; he's every-body's Joe. In addition to working long hours, he was the kind of dad to be the first to step up. At eight years old, I was denied the opportunity to play baseball in a neighboring town because their league rules prevented kids from outside their borders from playing there. The next day my dad founded Northport Little League. Since then, hundreds of kids have benefited from his and my mom's efforts. She was right there, too, securing sponsorships in town to help get the league off the ground. My parents live in a continuous state of helping other people. I can't keep up with the countless random acts of kindness that they have done for others. It was watching them model hard work and pay attention to the needs of other people that shaped me. As I said, they didn't lecture it. By just being the people they are, by modeling their values, they taught me. It was as if they said through their actions, "This is what our family is about."

Understand that your player is always watching what you do. If you talk about being on time for the workouts but you consistently show up late, your words ring hollow. If you bring no energy to the workout you are running, how can you expect the player to bring energy? If you are distracted during your workout, how can you ask for total focus from someone else? What's even more important to realize is that people—whether players, coworkers, or even our kids—all can sense when you're not sincere. If you say one thing and do something else, it erodes their trust and respect. And just because they haven't called you out on it doesn't mean that you've gotten away with something.

There is a saying that has become a golden nugget for me: "We teach people how to treat us." What does that mean? To me, it means that if you listen to others, they will listen to you. If you are always looking to help others, they will usually look to be helpful to you. If you respect others, they will be respectful of you. If you trust others, they will tend to trust you. Of course, there are no guarantees for this because all people are different, but why not take the lead? Show the behaviors you want others to use when they are with you. Don't just preach. Lead by example and demonstrate what you want the player to do.

Players (and, for that matter, everyone you interact with) are watching your behaviors and making decisions about you. They are not trying to figure out your intent. One of my favorite quotes is from Ralph Waldo Emerson, who said, "Who you are speaks so loudly I can't hear what you're saying." It is always your actions that truly speak for you.

How important is the personal makeup of the teacher in regard to their character? It's everything. It's foundational. You will never fully instill quality habits in your players if you don't embody them yourself.

> You will never fully instill quality habits in your players if you don't embody them yourself.

There is another concept at work here that I will do an even deeper dive into. It is that we can never give away something we don't have. If you do not have a dozen apples, how can you give them away? The answer is that you can't. As coaches and teachers, if we make a commitment to work to improve ourselves, we will have more to give away in every aspect of our teaching. What we feel and believe about ourselves is vital. Thousands of years ago, Socrates said that the key to living is always to learn how to live. As long as we feel that we are progressing, we will be constantly adding to our metaphorical apples.

KNOW YOURSELF

The process for setting the right example starts by making an open and honest assessment of our own strengths and weaknesses. Unfortunately, this is a step that many people skip because they don't see the importance of it or they don't want to go to the trouble. Plus, it isn't easy. Benjamin Franklin said that there are three things that are very hard: "steel, a diamond, and to know one's self."

There's a quick self-awareness exercise that I like to do when I am going to work with a player on a particular issue. I identify the issue to be addressed, then do an informal assessment of both the player and myself on that issue. I do this in my head, but it looks like this:

SKILL TO BE DEVELOPED: _____

PLAYER EFFECTIVENESS LEVEL				
1	2	3	4	5
Ineffective	Somewhat ineffective	Neutral	Somewhat effective	Effective

MY EFFECTIVENESS LEVEL				
1	2	3	4	5
Ineffective	Somewhat ineffective	Neutral	Somewhat effective	Effective

This is a useful approach to help anyone, not just a basketball player. We have to be clear about our own skill level in order to be helpful. If I find that I am at a lower level, what can I do to raise my game to be more helpful to the person? Here's an example that might apply to a manager helping a subordinate:

SKILL TO BE DEVELOPED: Interrupt coworkers less when they are speaking; listen more.

EMPLOYEE EFFECTIVENESS LEVEL				
1	2	3	4	5
Ineffective	Somewhat ineffective	Neutral	Somewhat effective	Effective

MY EFFECTIVENESS LEVEL				
1	2	3	4	5
Ineffective	Somewhat ineffective	Neutral	Somewhat effective	Effective

What do I need to do to develop myself before I can legitimately help someone else address the same issue? At North Carolina State University, I had the honor and privilege to play for legendary coach Jim Valvano. He placed a lot of emphasis on player self-awareness and self-esteem. He asked us two questions that I never forgot, and both addressed that all-important human component of self-esteem.

- Question 1: If you were a corporation, would you buy stock in yourself?

- Question 2: If you are in a room by yourself, do you enjoy the company?

How do you answer these questions? Again, the idea is to always work to improve yourself so that you have more to give away. That process has to start with an honest and open assessment of your own strengths and weaknesses.

CHAPTER 5

ESTABLISH A GROWTH MINDSET

Success is not an accident. Success is a choice.

—Stephen Curry

When Kobe Bryant died tragically in a helicopter crash in January 2020, it seemed like everybody being interviewed on the news had a Kobe story. Not surprisingly, most of these people described watching him play on one of the nights he accomplished some amazing basketball milestones. That made sense because Kobe was one of the best to ever play the game. He won five NBA championships and was an eighteen-time NBA All-Star in his twenty-year career with the Lakers. Then there was the night in 2006 when he scored eighty-one points in a single game. Only one player, Wilt Chamberlain, ever scored more points in a game.

THE MAMBA MINDSET

As gifted as Kobe was as an athlete, it wasn't his basketball prowess that I remember from my work with him in the summer of 1997. The thing that made a searing impression on me, and what differentiated Kobe from other people, was his thirst for success. Sure, his exceptional athletic skills got him into the NBA, but it was the mamba mindset that led him to become one of the best ever.

Prior to working with Kobe, I knew of him, but I did not know him personally. Kobe had just finished his rookie season, and Arn Tellem, the most powerful NBA agent at the time, represented him. Arn asked if I would work with Kobe on his shooting. We agreed that I would work with Kobe for eight days and then he would join the Lakers' summer league team. On that first day, Rob Palinka, who worked with Arn and who is now the GM of the LA Lakers, brought Kobe to the workout. Kobe and I got to work, and I was immediately impressed with his level of focus and concentration. My longtime friend and individual workout guru, David Thorpe, once told me he noticed that the great players listened with their eyes. That was definitely true for Kobe.

Technically speaking, Kobe shot a line drive with a whole bunch of movement that I knew was unnecessary. After a few minutes of shooting one foot from the basket, Kobe started to lock in. The increased arc and shorter motion began to feel comfortable to him, and I could see him getting energized by the results. As our scheduled ninety-minute workout was coming to an end, four guys were loosening up on the sideline for their workout with me. As the other players stepped onto the court, Kobe asked if he could stay and go through another workout with this new group.

In that second workout with NBA veterans, Kobe's intensity blew them away. His level of energy compared to these fresh players wasn't even close. As the second workout ended, like before, the small group for my third workout was getting ready to come onto the court. Once again, Kobe asked me if he could stay and train with this group. And once again, Kobe's level of effort and intensity was by far the best in the group.

This pattern continued for seven days straight. Kobe was the hardest worker and most intense player in every workout every time. We had one more workout on a Sunday, which was our eighth straight day, and he was feeling great about his shot. When we finished that day, Kobe and I walked out of the old Men's Gym together toward our cars. As we crossed UCLA's brick commons, I was so impressed by Kobe's work ethic that I felt compelled to tell him so. "Kobe, I'm probably not telling you something you don't already know, but if you keep working as hard as you do, you will be one of the best players to ever play this game."

Kobe almost stopped me midsentence, but he let me finish. Then, with an intense look in his eyes and conviction in his voice, he said, "No! I am going to be *the* best to ever play the game." Kobe, a player who had started only six games and played just fifteen minutes his first year in the league, made that proclamation. As a coach and as someone who has spent his whole life helping people to develop their skills, I realized in that moment that the tables were turned and that I was the one learning something. Kobe was already thirsty, and he was showing me the highest level of the growth mindset I had ever seen—a maniacal intensity toward perfection.

As fate would have it, Kobe proceeded to shoot horribly for that summer league. It's a common result in any sport that if you make changes to technique and you do not have time to fully ingrain the change in your mind and muscle memory, you will be caught between two different techniques the first time you jump into real competition, and it will get ugly. Temporarily. There is a short-term drop of effectiveness, but players will regain their existing level, then over time perform much better in the long run. It's only after quality repetition after quality repetition, building up that specific myelin pathway in the brain, that you will see real progress. That is what Kobe did, and his record speaks for itself.

My experience with the mamba mentality doesn't end there. I was hired as a coach for the Phoenix Suns two years later, and the team had a good year. We won fifty-three games and beat San Antonio in the first round of the playoffs. Our second-round opponent was the Lakers and none other than Kobe Bryant. We lost game one in LA. In game two, we were ahead by one point with 3.9 seconds left. Kobe got the ball and hit a turnaround jump shot with Jason Kidd draped all over him. Instead of going back to Phoenix 1–1, Kobe ripped our hearts out, and we headed back home down 2–0. The Lakers beat us in game three, then we came back and won game four. We headed back to LA and lost game five. Our season was over, and the Lakers went on to win the championship that year.

Less than a week after the Lakers cut down the nets, I went to LA before summer league started to visit some friends. I arrived on a Friday evening and decided to get in a workout. A friend of mine managed the Venice Gold's Gym, so I headed over there. When I walked into that gym on a Friday night at around eight o'clock, who did I see lathered in sweat but Kobe Bryant. He was not out celebrating, painting the town, and enjoying the accolades of the Lakers' championship. He was locked in and focused on improving from last season so that he could be even better. That was the mamba mentality, the growth mindset of a champion.

CHAMPIONS ARE OBSESSED WITH GETTING BETTER

Instilling the mindset of constant improvement is not a new concept, but it's a mentality that must be fully ingrained as you develop your relationship with your player. Every fiber of your being must demonstrate to the student that your only focus is for them to constantly improve. Stephen Covey refers to this in his classic book *The 7 Habits of Highly Effective People* as *sharpening the saw*, the seventh habit.[7] Best-selling author and thought leader Tony Robbins calls it *CANI*, which stands for Constant and Never-Ending Improvement.[8] Both authors make the case for never being satisfied with the status quo.

There is a legend about Socrates that tells the story of one of his students. The student constantly hounded Socrates about reaching his level of knowledge. He would follow Socrates around everywhere and would ask him over and over, "Teacher, how can I gain your wisdom?"

One day Socrates took his student down to the river and told him to walk into the water until it reached his waist. Socrates then told the student to get on his knees, and the student immediately complied. Socrates grabbed the student by the neck and pushed his head under the water. At first, the student remained calm because over the years he had come to trust Socrates. As time passed, the student's trust waned and he started to struggle. Socrates continued to hold the student's head under the water. It soon reached a point when the student lost all trust and was flailing and twisting in panic to break free. At that point Socrates allowed the student's head to pop

---

7   Stephen R. Covey, *The 7 Habits of Highly Effective People: Powerful Lessons in Personal Change* (New York: Free Press, 1989).

8   Anthony Robbins, *Giant Steps: Small Changes to Make a Big Difference* (New York: Simon & Shuster, 1994).

above the water. As the student coughed and gasped for air, Socrates asked the student, "When you were under water, what did you want more than anything else?"

The student responded, "Air!"

Socrates told the student, "When you seek wisdom like you sought your next breath, you will find it."

THE GROWTH MINDSET

In Carol Dweck's best seller *Mindset*, she establishes that there are two ways of thinking.[9] One is a *fixed* mindset in which the thinking is, *That's just the way it is. I'm not smart enough or skilled enough, or I have nothing to gain other than being who I am right now.* In comparison, Dweck points out that with a *growth mindset*, the way of thinking is that anything is possible if we work hard and smart toward our goal.

During my first year in the NBA, Scott Skiles replaced Danny Ainge as head coach for the Suns. Scott was a natural as an NBA coach. His strength was teaching and making players accountable on defense, and he was brilliant at it. For the first two seasons under Scott, we were a top-five defensive team. Early in the season during my first year, I noticed that nobody on our staff was charting our offense. It would have been easy for me to just watch the game, talk to the players when I felt there was a need, or just sit there and pay attention. But I wanted to grow and increase the amount of quality input if I could. As a result, I started charting every offensive possession and its effectiveness in order to be helpful to the team and the coaches. That did two things for me. One, it allowed me to get a deeper understanding of our effectiveness on both offense and

---

9   Carol S. Dweck, *Mindset: The New Psychology of Success* (New York: Ballantine Books, 2016).

defense. Two, it helped me create a mindset that was open to all the other elements of the game that could have an impact. Just like when you are working with a player on their skill development and you are locked in and laser-focused on certain things, you begin to make connections as well as distinctions. You add more dots, so to speak, and by doing so, you are able to continually connect more dots. I experienced that this level of focus also opened me up to venture outside the box of what has been the norm and allowed my creative process to be fully engaged. Having a growth mindset makes it easier to see efficiencies and the need for constant improvement. One of the things that charting illustrated to me in Phoenix during our 2003–2004 season was that our smaller lineup (usually Shawn Marion and Amar'e Stoudemire at forward and center, respectively) charted very well. Mike D'Antoni, at the time a fellow assistant, and I would have many conversations about the lineup's effect on the game. The following year, Mike was the head coach, and we implemented that lineup during our training camp. Little did we know that it would lead us to attain the best record in the NBA regular season and to make it all the way to the Western Conference Finals.

Maintaining a growth mindset opens the door for constant improvement. There are many business examples of how this has worked effectively. One of my favorites comes from the story of rebuilding war-ravaged Japan after World War II. In 1951, an American engineer was credited with being mainly responsible for the Japanese postwar business miracle. William Edwards Deming, a statistician, engineer, and professor, visited Japan and helped instill in the Japanese culture this

> Maintaining a growth mindset opens the door for constant improvement.

idea of constant improvement. At that time, it was small companies like Sony and Toyota that adopted Deming's concepts. There is now a Deming award, and the Japanese created a single word for this concept: *kaizen*.

How do you instill this growth mindset and openness to constant improvement into your workouts? It all comes down to maintaining a moment-by-moment focus. Coaching is about emphasizing. It involves constantly looking at ways to improve, then stating, showing, and restating. You have to vary your message because all players are different—something I will emphasize many times in this book. This means that what and how you're saying and teaching something may resonate with one person but could seem like a foreign language to another person. Find a way to instill this mindset and reinforce it every day.

What are some signs that a player has a fixed mindset? You will hear them say things like "I tried that. Doesn't work. That will never work for me. Why mess with it?" You work to instill in them that they need to try something different to get better. Some players want to work only on their strengths because it is easier and more fun. It's hard to work on their weaknesses because they don't want to go through the pain, frustration, and boredom related to the improvements they have to make. Unless you embrace it, you don't get through it. A player with a growth mindset, by comparison, will say things like "What's next? What else can I try?" As Carol Dweck states, "We like to think of our champions and idols as superheroes who were born different from us. We don't like to think of them as relatively ordinary people who made themselves extraordinary."[10]

For anyone in the process of achieving a goal, the growth mindset is about understanding that they aren't there yet and that

10   Ibid.

they need to continue to push toward it. Dr. Andrew Huberman, a highly acclaimed neuroscientist from Stanford University, breaks down the chemical process involved. He explains that during the process of achieving a goal, there is something called a *subjective dopamine secretion*. If we are able to control the *how* and the *when* of our dopamine secretion as we fight through the stress and frustration of reaching a goal, the pleasure of the dopamine we feel in the process will allow us to power through to our goal.

I believe that I experienced this phenomenon when I was training for the New York City Marathon. Two months before the race, I ran almost every day, and every Sunday I added to my run to make sure that I ran progressively farther each week. I guess it was that dopamine hit that I was feeling after every Sunday run. I was always excited to hop in my car and drive my running route to clock the mileage for that day. The longest training run I completed was 17 miles before I ran the full 26.2 miles in the marathon. It was those feelings of progress every Sunday that enabled me to build up and to grow in my conditioning. This ultimately led me to achieve my goal.

CHAPTER 6

CREATE THE VISION

Begin with the end in mind.

—Stephen Covey

What is the end result you're looking for? What are your expectations? What is it going to take to become the player, the student, or the skilled professional you want to be? Most people wouldn't start out on a trip without knowing where they want to end up. A coach must be able to articulate and communicate the shared destination for the developmental journey, and the player needs to be able to visualize what that will look like when they get there.

THE IMPORTANCE OF CLEAR GOALS

The vision itself should be challenging. Edwin Locke and Gary Latham are the gurus of goal attainment research in the social sciences. Their studies indicate that setting challenging goals—stretch goals—caused people to have more success than easy goals.[11] Easy goals became tedious and demotivating. By comparison, accomplishing a difficult goal motivated the person to continue to achieve even more. In Kobe Bryant's case, his vision was that he was going to be the best to ever play the game. Every moment of every day, he kept that vision locked into his psyche. The level of a player's focus on their vision will be proportional to their ability to maximize their skill and get close to, but hopefully never fully arrive at, the vision they have established. That vision will continually pull them toward the level of greatness they seek.

KNOW WHAT SUCCESS LOOKS LIKE

As a coach, you can use the vision you and the player establish at the start of your working relationship together. This vision will help greatly and will allow you to fuel the intensity level of every single workout. In Phoenix, we were fortunate to get super talented Joe Johnson from the Celtics in 2001–2002, the middle of his rookie season. That became the beginning of a three-and-a-half-year relationship in which Joe and I worked out together almost every day. We established (half-jokingly because Joe is so humble) that we wanted him to have the purest, sweetest-looking jump shot in the NBA. We also had a vision that Joe would become the most fundamentally sound player in the league. Period. As a result, each day we began by

---

11   Edwin A. Locke and Gary P. Latham, "Building a Practically Useful Theory of Goal Setting and Task Motivation," *American Psychologist* 57, no. 9 (2002): 705–17.

working intensively on every aspect of the game. We used a variety of approaches every day, but all were designed to reinforce the shared vision we held for Joe.

The 2003–2004 season was not a good one for the Suns. We made a blockbuster trade with the Knicks to create an abundant supply of cap room for the summer, and one result was that we finished with only twenty-nine wins. That summer we used the cap space to pick up supreme point guard Steve Nash from Dallas and tough gunslinger wing Quentin Richardson from the Clippers. We added these veterans to the talented young core of Amar'e Stoudemire, Shawn Marion, Leandro Barbosa, and Joe Johnson. That group of players, combined with Coach Mike D'Antoni's belief system, made magic happen. In 2004–2005, which would turn out to be Joe Johnson's last season in Phoenix, the Suns had a breakout year and a 62–20 record. That was the best record in the NBA and gave us the home court advantage throughout the playoffs. That year during the Western Conference Semifinals against Dallas, Joe, one of our most durable players, went up and landed off balance, falling on his face and fracturing an orbital bone. We got past the Mavericks and made it to the Western Conference Finals. But with Joe out the first three games, we ultimately lost to San Antonio. It's probably spilled milk, but I firmly believe that if we had Joe healthy the whole series, we would have a championship ring from that year.

The primary reason Joe became a member of the all-rookie team, a seven-time All-Star, was due to his incredible focus and daily work habits. He never lost sight of his vision of the player he wanted to become. A couple of critical factors came into play to help the incredible shooting results from that 2004–2005 season. Joe shot 48 percent from three-point range, and many said that Joe's form was picture perfect. Just liked he envisioned it.

THE PSYCHOLOGY OF DEVELOPMENT

As you and the player work to create a vision, something that goes hand in hand with this process is the player's underlying belief system. In the classic book *Think and Grow Rich*, which is maybe one of the best books ever written on the philosophy of success, the essence of Napoleon Hill's message is the following: "What a man can conceive and believe, he can achieve."[12] Another illustration of this comes from what is thought to be one of the oldest poems on competition titled "Thinking" by Walter D. Wintle. The poem so powerfully states, "Life's battles don't always go to the stronger or faster man; / But sooner or later the person who wins is the one who thinks he can!"[13] What we believe about our capabilities means everything, and it is the coach's job to be a builder of belief. There is no greater thing in life than to really believe in someone and then to have them start to believe in themselves. There is an endless list of lives that have been changed for the better in every way because of a coach or mentor who truly believed in them.

> What we believe about our capabilities means everything, and it is the coach's job to be a builder of belief.

How do you change your belief system? It has been one of my life's quests to continually get a deeper understanding of that topic. It is such an important aspect of the learning process that volumes have been written about it. For the sake of this book, I will touch on what I consider to be the main points.

---

12 Napoleon Hill, *Think and Grow Rich* (Meridien, CT: The Ralston Society,1937).

13 Walter D. Wintle, *Unity* (Lees Summit, MO: Unity Tract Society, 1905).

As Denis Waitley stated in his best-selling book *The Psychology of Winning*, success is directly related to a person's self-talk.[14] Right now, as you read this book, you are thinking to yourself in six hundred to eight hundred words per minute. Try to stop thinking for fifteen seconds. You can't. Of those thoughts, many are habitual. Ask yourself, "Are my thoughts empowering or disempowering?"

The key is to find the door to your subconscious mind and to observe all the players' language and reactions. The first step toward change is awareness. Help your player recognize when they stray into that negative minefield. Make them aware that many times we play CDs in our heads. One situation leads to a string of related thoughts from the past. The secret is understanding that fact, becoming aware of when it happens, and choosing not to play that CD.

It should be the coach's job to give the player at least a workable, surface-level knowledge of how the mind functions and how important it is to the process—to constantly remind them in many different ways. Again, all players are different, so always look for what best resonates with that player.

What can the player start to do? The first step toward change and growth is always awareness. They can begin to pay attention to their thoughts and to incorporate positive affirmations into their day with the corresponding feeling. The feeling is critical. Our minds cannot differentiate from what happens to us and what is vividly imagined.

THE QUEST FOR GREATNESS

Over the years, I have given out hundreds of copies of Og Mandino's book *The Greatest Salesman in the World* to players, friends, and

---

14 Denis Waitley, *The Psychology of Winning: Ten Qualities of a Total Winner* (New York: Berkley Books, 1984).

strangers alike.[15] Why? Because it changed my life and trajectory. The book is a short, beautiful story with ten scrolls at the end. Mandino describes how to unlock the magic of the scrolls by reading each one three times a day for thirty days.

After following those instructions and living with that book, those scrolls are now part of the software of my mind. Each scroll empowers you in a different part of your mindset. It wasn't until a year or so after I finished the ten months of living with the scrolls that I looked back through the book and realized why my intensity grew whenever a player used the words *can't* or *tired*. It is because the third scroll states, "I will persist until I succeed." It also states that words such as *impossible* or *can't* will be stricken from my vocabulary. I know for certain that it has changed the way I think and therefore the way I see the world.

I believe that the greatest power a person has is the power to choose. Kobe said that greatness was a choice. You must choose greatness, which means doing all the hard work that goes along with it as well as sacrificing moments with your family and friends. Greatness might take you away from a balanced life.

How do you define greatness? One person might see it as having a balance in life that includes a deep and loving relationship with their family and friends. Maybe being able to contribute to the community and still be able to provide for their family's needs. Another sees it as the singular focus on being the ultimate athlete in their sport. Is it possible to have both? That is a real and powerful question that professionals with big hearts ask themselves every single day. I don't assume to know how that player defines greatness before I discuss it with them. It is one of the reasons why I emphasize a holistic approach to player development.

---

15   Og Mandino, *The Greatest Salesman in the World* (New York: Bantam Books, 1983).

Another way to rewire our minds toward our vision is to meditate. I have started meditating only in the last couple of years, but I believe that my life would be inherently different if I had begun this practice earlier. In his book *Breaking the Habit of Being Yourself*, Joe Dispenza notes that if we are always getting all our information from our senses, then we are always living in the past.[16] Ninety-five percent of what you do is habitual. You wake up, brush your teeth, get your coffee, and drive to work, all without a thought because these actions are habitual. When do you create new thoughts? Dispenza argues that if you are sitting in a room in silence, with your eyes closed and your body completely still, new thoughts will be created in your mind. I go into more detail about the practical application of meditation in chapter 24.

---

16 Joe Dispenza, *Breaking the Habit of Being Yourself: How to Lose Your Mind and Create a New One* (Carlsbad, CA: Hay House, 2013).

CHAPTER 7

TAKE THE TIME TO TEACH

If you have an important point to make, don't try to be subtle or clever. Use a pile driver. Hit the point once. Then come back and hit it again. Then hit it a third time—a tremendous whack.

—Winston Churchill

"Phil, we would love to keep you on staff, but we have a new head coach coming in, and he will want to bring in all his own assistants." This was the conversation I had with the athletic director at the University of Florida on October 31, 1989. The Gators' head coach, Norm Sloan, was forced to leave two weeks after the season started. How could this be happening? We had won the SEC championship the previous year, and we had everyone back. It did happen to be Halloween. Was this trick-or-treat?

I went back to my condo and was met there by crews from three local TV stations waiting for a comment. I went inside, and my roommates jokingly asked me if I was going to pretend to be a basketball coach for Halloween. Tough crowd! The next morning my roommates left and went about their normal day, and I sat down in an empty condo to figure out my next move. The season had already started, and every coach understands that our profession is like musical chairs. Unfortunately for me, the music was off and all jobs were filled for the season, so it was too late to get a coaching position somewhere else. This was my first up-close look at real adversity. I sat there, alone, pondering my direction: *This is good, but why?* I asked myself an empowering question: How can I make this the greatest year of my life? That question took my mind in an exciting direction.

WHEN IN DOUBT, CREATE A PLAN

It occurred to me that I had no ties in Gainesville except my good friends, and I was still being paid by the University of Florida. I decided to create my own basketball university per se, touring the country and absorbing as much knowledge as I could about coaching basketball. I would do that by reaching out to everyone I knew (pre-email!). I packed up and set out to visit sixteen different universities. I watched practices, talked with coaches and players, and generally took in as much as I could. I also renewed my connections with guys I knew from my own basketball journey. One of those people was Mark Gottfried, who had been a player at Alabama. Mark was now an assistant at UCLA under Jim Harrick, so I was sure to make that university one of my destinations. (Little did I know that I would end up back on campus years later working out with the players I mentioned in chapter 1.) Mark was not only kind enough to make it possible for me to watch their practices all week but also got me a ticket to the Bruins game that weekend.

When I got to Pauley Pavilion for the game, I walked in during warm-ups and headed down to my seat. I looked up and realized that fifty feet in front of me stood one of my heroes, former UCLA coach John Wooden. I said to myself, *Phil, you idiot. You're traveling the country to learn as much about the game as possible and there is Coach Wooden, one of the best ever.* I walked down to where he was standing and got in line to say hello. When my turn came, I said, "Coach, my name's Phil Weber. I coached with Norm Sloan." I knew Coach Wooden would recognize Coach Sloan's name because he lost to Sloan in the semifinals of the 1974 NCAA tournament. I thought I needed to drop a name to make a connection for Coach Wooden. I learned later that it didn't make any difference. I said, "Coach, I would love to spend some time talking with you."

One of the winningest coaches in college basketball pulled out a piece of paper, wrote down his name and phone number, handed it to me, and said, "Call me on Monday, Phil."

OFF TO SEE THE WIZARD OF WESTWOOD

I called him from a pay phone at ten o'clock that Monday morning. When he answered, I said, "Coach, this is Phil Weber. I'd love to ask you some basketball questions I've been thinking about."

He said, "Sure, Phil, come on over at one." He gave me directions to his condo in Encino, then we hung up. Suddenly I realized that I had no idea what I was going to ask him. I walked to a Burger King around the corner and wrote out twelve questions that I really wanted to learn about basketball.

John Wooden was the most articulate, humble, and learned man I've ever met. His influence on me from our meeting is one of the reasons why I started to write poems. Coach Wooden used poetry as a kind of shorthand. He seemed to appreciate how the exact right word or spare phrase could summarize so much. When I asked him about facing adversity, he recited, "When I look back, it seems to me all the grief that had to be left me when the pain was over, stronger than I was before." I was blown away. The one that stays with me the most is about setting an example: "No written word or spoken plea can teach the youth what they ought to be, nor all the books on all the shelves. But it's what the teachers are themselves." You lead by example. And that connects to another of his quotes: "You can never demand respect. You command respect with who you are."

THE HEART OF A TEACHER

He offered me a lot in our conversation and patiently answered my questions. I had always known about Coach Wooden from his coaching record, most notably his unprecedented ten NCAA championships. But that afternoon in 1990 opened my eyes to the importance of the coach as teacher. More than that, sitting in his living room as he gave generously of his time to me, someone he had never met before the previous weekend, instilled in me the drive to pay it forward—to give without the expectation of return.

This was an event that changed me forever, and I remember so much about him and how he treated me that day. As I was leaving, I told him, "Coach Valvano would always say, 'Life boils down to very few moments,' and for me, this has been one of those moments. Thank you." I was so touched by how willing he was to give his time to me with no expectation of getting anything from it himself. I didn't know how to thank him enough, but I had his address, so I sent him a Harry and David fruit basket later that day. I flew back to Gainesville the next day, and on Thursday, two days later, I checked my mailbox to find a note from Coach Wooden. I opened it to read, "Dear Phil. Although it is often used without real feeling, when used with sincerity, no collection of words can be more meaningful or expressive." Then a simple "Thanks, John Wooden."

In the years since, I have found many, many, many people who had that same experience with him that I did. He just wanted to help. Just like there are Kobe Bryant stories, there are John Wooden stories. What that tells me is that all the great ones leave similar impressions and that's why they're great. He helped me understand that life exists on many levels. Communicating with players requires an understanding of where they are, on what level. It requires coaches to understand their own level and to be aware of matching the player's level. Mostly I remember his level of humility and how sincere he was. He just wanted to help.

WHEN YOU TEACH, EXPLAIN THE WHY

I try to pay forward the time that coaches like John Wooden have given to me by really being a teacher for my players. When I work with athletes, I want them to have a deep understanding of what we are doing. It is my belief that if you are teaching fundamentals, it is imperative that the player not only knows the what but also the why. When working with a younger player or one new to me, I have a way to demonstrate the importance of quickness and speed that comes from an athletic position. The player is usually standing up, listening to what I am saying. I slowly walk over to them, tell them to hold their arms straight out to the side, and then I push the player hard in the chest. They always fall backward, unbalanced. I then ask them to bend at the knees and waist while keeping their arms tight to their body and I push them again. Invariably, they are more balanced and hardly move because they have engaged their core to provide them with optimal balance. A coach can tell players many things, but showing them helps them understand and remember.

> A coach can tell players many things, but showing them helps them understand and remember.

All players are different, so the messages you use will evolve from getting to know them and their learning styles. In chapter 3, I mentioned that we acquired Boris Diaw in the trade for Joe Johnson. Those two players had very different learning styles, and I had to adjust my coaching to be most helpful in their development. Joe had a quiet personality. He accepted what we were doing, dug right in, and worked hard. Boris had a very different personality. He would take my instruction and suggestions, but in many cases he wanted me to explain why we were doing it. I was told that Boris's nickname was *Oui mais*, which in French means "Yes but." I saw his ability and potential, and I understood that he wasn't challenging my instruction; he just wanted to know why he was doing something.

When working with another super talented young player for the Phoenix Suns, Amar'e Stoudemire, we started to focus intensively on his shot. If you analyzed Amar'e's shot as a rookie, you would say that it was less than perfect. He never had the same timing on his release. For Amar'e, it wasn't an issue of missing left or right. Rather, his shot was usually short or long. I believe that players should try to simplify a movement or action when possible. Why? Two reasons. First, fewer movements result in quicker total action (and the most important aspect for a basketball player is quickness). Second, it is easier to lock into repeatable mechanics if there are fewer moving parts.

As a teacher, how do you get Amar'e to remember and adopt a simpler form on his shot? First you explain to him your analysis of why you believe he is missing shots. Show him on the court in slower motion. Use video of him shooting in slow motion and show him all the details that you feel are most important. Once you help him establish a vision of the end result, explain the process in depth of how to get there. Remember that throughout this discussion, you must explain the why.

Now it's time to get to the work of instilling perfect form. The next step that I use with players is to create a mantra that is unique to their developmental challenge to help them mentally lock in. In Amar'e's case, I also threw a little ego-building into his mantra. I explained that he needed a "clutch" for his shot, meaning that he needed to have the same starting point for every shot. The mantra we created came as a result of a question I asked Amar'e: "How will anybody ever take a picture of your perfect form if you don't use that clutch pause?" We developed the following mantra: "Jump up, take a picture, follow through." I would constantly repeat his mantra during all our workouts together. The goal is not only to drill the physical aspect of the shot to muscle memory but also to have the mantra sink deep into the player's subconscious mind. Was this mantra successful for Amar'e? You'll find out in chapter 13.

Daniel Coyle, author of the book *The Talent Code*, explains this well.[17] He describes how the combination of practice, motivation, and coaching work together to stimulate the brain's development of connective myelin. This myelin can greatly increase the speed and accuracy of a player's movements and thought processing. To help

---

17 Daniel Coyle, *The Talent Code: Greatest Isn't Born. It's Grown. Here's How.*
(London: Arrow Books, 2010).

players visualize the concept of myelin, I describe it as a steel cable. An extremely important aspect of improvement, once you learn the correct way, is to be focused every time. I explained that to Amar'e, and I used one of my favorite metaphors. I told Amar'e that now that he had a form and rhythm that gave him success, he must be focused and disciplined to shoot it that way every time. Each time he shot using the new effective way, he placed a strand that began to form a new cable. If he walked out onto the court during warm-ups and started throwing up shots the old way, he was taking off strands of that steel cable.

Early in the process, I would watch Amar'e from a place where he couldn't see me. He would invariably lose focus and start shooting the old way. I would sneak up on him and ask, loudly and intensely, "What are you doing? What are you doing?"

He usually responded, "What do you mean?"

I would say, "You just took off twelve strands of your steel cable! How are you going to get the shot you want if you are not one hundred percent disciplined and locked in?" Over time those interactions became less frequent until the steel cable of his new shooting form was locked in.

Amar'e was a gifted learner, and he picked up things quickly. We began our work midway through the 2003–2004 season, and he locked in and trained hard all summer. I committed to being wherever he was to continue his progress. Amar'e's dedication and focus really paid off. His ability to make an elbow jump shot made him almost unguardable. He quickly moved up to averaging an efficient twenty-six points per game.

Daniel Coyle notes an important and predictable phenomenon. Before creating myelin, there is always an uncomfortable growth period. It involves moving through the pain and boredom to reach greatness, which is a serious commitment. As an example, he points out that many people think that Michelangelo was born gifted. The reality is that he had a hammer in his hand, practicing sculpture, before he could read. People have no idea how hard he worked to become so accomplished. That is the perspective of the growth mindset, and it is the place we try to get to with players—the understanding on the other side of awareness.

In his best-selling book *Start with Why*, Simon Sinek shows just how powerful that question is.[18] The question *why* a player plays the game can really be helpful in establishing a deeper relationship with them and, just as important, can determine the right motivational button to keep them engaged.

If you simply ask a player to do something, they will have a surface-level understanding of your request. But if you consistently take the time to explain why you are doing a certain action or drill, that level of understanding goes much deeper. Younger players may have only a limited ability to understand the deeper details. But as you work with more experienced players, explaining the why is imperative. In my experience, this has been particularly important when working with players in the NBA to establish trust and clear expectations. You should strive to give them as deep an understanding as you possibly can.

It's my job as a coach who is trying to help a player get better to not only keep them empowered but also keep them empowered toward perfection. We might know that we will never get there, but we will get as close as we can. We're never perfect, but we're striving for that, and it's a beautiful journey when the player understands not only the goal but also the why. As Coach Wooden said, "It's what you learn after you know it all that counts."

---

18   Simon Sinek, *Start with Why: How Great Leaders Inspire Everyone to Take Action* (New York: Penguin Group, 2009).

CHAPTER 8

CREATE A CULTURE OF ACCOUNTABILITY

There are only two options regarding commitment. You're either in or you're out. There's no such thing as life in-between.

—Pat Riley

Our idea of a positive culture starts at a young age. Although I wouldn't have described it using these terms now, I realize that I was lucky to have experienced strong team culture early in my basketball career. I attended Long Island Lutheran High School. The head basketball coach there was Reverend Ed Visscher. He was a legendary coach whose teams were regularly ranked nationally, and we played a schedule that rivaled some small colleges. The cornerstone of our team culture was hard work. He demonstrated it himself and insisted on it from his teams. He was quoted once in an article in *Forbes* that other teams overestimated the impact of size. "It's not how big you are, it's how good you are."[19] There's not much a player can control about getting bigger, but there is a whole lot that they can control about developing their skills.

That lesson was reinforced to me once when I was discussing my theory about culture with NBA All-Star Jamal Mashburn. He told me about his son's pathway to Brewster Academy, a prep school. He explained how different it was from the other schools he attended and how much he improved with a better structure and in a better-coached environment.

CULTURE IS CONTAGIOUS

In the NBA today, every team has great facilities. Most teams have five or six player development coaches, a G League team, and technologies to help players develop. Coaches know that it is part of their jobs to develop players and to ultimately win, so I've been incubated in excellent developmental environments for a long time. But it hasn't always been like that.

I remember what some people told me in 1999 when they heard I was going to work for the Suns. They said that it wasn't exactly a super intense environment. I didn't pay any attention to what people said. I went to Phoenix with an open mind and a determination to work as hard as I could; I wanted to take advantage of this tremendous opportunity that Danny Ainge and Jerry and Bryan Colangelo gave me. What I found in Phoenix was a strong family culture geared

---

19   Tom Van Riper, "The NBA's Most Overpaid Players" *Forbes*, October 23, 2009, https://www.forbes.com/2009/10/22/overpaid-basketball-players-business-sports-nba.html#1478dbf85f9e.

toward determining what was needed to ultimately win. I continued the teaching and player development the same way that I had been doing it for years, with two exceptions. My skill development was now focused around and specifically geared toward team concepts. Plus, I now had other responsibilities that I didn't have at the Men's Gym at UCLA.

During my time with the Phoenix Suns, we had a well-respected strength coach named Robin Pound, who had a knack for giving people nicknames. As a result of the players' reaction to my intense and detailed workouts, he started calling me Drill Phil. The name stuck, and many of those players from my first four years in Phoenix still call me that when they see me now. Did I have an impact on the environment? That's hard to say because we had some players who were exceptionally hard workers, like Rodney Rogers, a seasoned vet looking to have a breakout season, and Shawn Marion, the ninth pick in the draft from UNLV. The one thing I knew for sure, every day, was that I controlled the intensity level of all my workouts.

TAKE THE LONG VIEW

My journey of working with and learning from great coaches and players continued when I left Phoenix at the end of the 2007–2008 season and joined the staff of the New York Knicks. When head coach Mike D'Antoni and the rest of our staff arrived in New York, we were all on board with Knicks president Donnie Walsh's strategy. His plan was to clear cap space during our first two seasons in order to take the long-range view and go after blue-chip players in the free agent class of 2010, including first and foremost LeBron James. In 2008, we initiated a deal with the Clippers to get starting shooting guard Cuttino Mobley, who had eighteen points the game before the trade. We traded Zach Randolph and Mardy Collins and picked up Cuttino and Tim Thomas. We finally had an exceptional true two-guard for our system, and we were building. Or so we thought. In Cuttino's physical, they discovered that he had a condition known as hypertrophic cardiomyopathy. This was the same condition that afflicted Hank Gathers and Reggie Lewis. No problem. Just cancel the deal, right? Nope—because Cuttino's money came off at the end of the year, we still executed the trade. Cuttino retired technically as a Knick, but he never played a game in New York.

In 2010, we had our sights firmly set on free agents LeBron James, Dwyane Wade, Amar'e Stoudemire, and Chris Bosh, to name a few. It was a big class, and we were financially positioned for it. When the dust settled from free agency, the Big Three ended up in Miami, and we landed our super talented and familiar center, Amar'e Stoudemire. People forget that in his first season with the Knicks, Amar'e had a record nine straight games of thirty points to help us win fourteen out of sixteen in December 2010. Things were coming together nicely. We were successful enough to acquire Carmelo Anthony from the Denver Nuggets, and we made the playoffs in our third year but ended up losing to the Boston Celtics in the first round.

We continued to rebuild in New York and to develop the players we had through the next two seasons. Despite our first two seasons ending in losing records, only getting to the playoffs in our third season, Coach D'Antoni and the rest of the staff knew from the start that we were taking the long view in building a team in New York. Which leads us to the 2011–2012 season—and what a season it was!

THE IMPORTANCE OF NETWORK

The 2011–2012 season got off to a strange nonstart. It began with a lockout that reduced the season from eighty-two games to sixty-six and delayed the start until December 2011. In the meantime, our Knicks coaching staff reported to the practice facility every day during the lockout to prepare for whenever the games would resume. There was only so much training we could do and then it became counterproductive because we really didn't know our team yet. After preparation, it becomes adjusting and modifying because you never nail everything 100 percent. We used to plan an entire week in advance of training camp, but sometimes the defense is ahead of the offense, or vice versa. All that preparation time was wasted because the team we believed we had was not the team we actually had, and we wouldn't know that until they started playing.

We finished preparing as much as we could, and Mike D'Antoni said that the coaches might as well take the weekends off for the rest of the lockout. I decided to head to Miami to visit friends, and the highlight was dinner with two longtime friends. One was Steve Stowe, vice president of the Miami Heat, and the other was Heat head coach Erik Spoelstra (or Spo). For five hours we sat at a restaurant called Hakkasan on the top floor of the Fontainebleau hotel and discussed basketball, philosophy, and life.

I came back from that trip with a deeper understanding of a quality culture. It is generally accepted around the NBA that when people talk about quality championship cultures, two teams are always in that discussion. One is the San Antonio Spurs, and the other is the Miami Heat. I cannot speak in depth about San Antonio, but like many, or possibly all, coaches in the NBA, I admire the quality and the consistency of what the Spurs culture has accomplished. What is also apparent is the success of the people who previously played with the Spurs, such as Danny Ferry with Cleveland and Atlanta, Sam Presti in OKC, Sean Marks in Brooklyn, Dennis Lindsey in Utah, and Mike Budenholzer in Milwaukee; Steve Kerr also gives credit to Coach Popovich for much of what he's done for Golden State. I did, however, have the absolute good fortune to spend time on and around the coaching staff of the Miami Heat, but more on that story later.

CULTURAL FIT IS CRITICAL

During the lockout, we made a substantial change to our team dynamics by amnestying our starting point guard, Chauncey Billups, and signing center Tyson Chandler fresh off his championship season in Dallas. Due to the lockout, our entire training camp lasted only five days. Normally it lasted a month, including eight preseason games.

We learned so much about the makeup of that 2011–2012 team, including the discovery that our New York skyline starting lineup of Carmelo Anthony, Amar'e Stoudemire, and Tyson Chandler turned out to be a challenging fit for the changing NBA that we helped to create in Phoenix. The shortened training camp meant that we had little time to figure that out. Our first two years were a turnstile of players coming and going to position us financially. In the run-up to 2012, I coached sixty-three different players with the Knicks.

We were able to deliver the Knicks fans a playoff team in year three, but we were now facing some difficult issues. As I stated, we had amnestied Chauncey Billups to get Tyson Chandler. Chauncey had started for us at the point guard spot the previous year, but he was getting toward the end of his tremendous seventeen-year career. In Tyson Chandler, we were getting a top defensive presence and lob threat, but we were entering our season without a tested point guard, which was a major question mark.

LINSANITY IN THE BIG APPLE

The world will remember that special time in New York and in NBA history when an unknown Harvard grad and little-used reserve lit up the city. Jeremy Lin didn't get much court time for the Knicks until he cracked the starting lineup in February 2012 and then the Knicks won seven games in a row with him at point. Jeremy made it onto the cover of *Sports Illustrated* and the Knicks made it to the playoffs. What a great run! The way that team was playing was a thing of beauty, and the Knicks had the best defense in the league. There is no question for me, however, that that was the beginning of the end.

We were all caught off guard when, on March 15, 2012, while driving home from a shootaround, Mike D'Antoni decided to resign. I had been with Mike for ten years, first in Phoenix and then in New York. Glen Grunwald, the Knicks general manager at the time, called and told me that Mike Woodson would get the head coaching job and that he had some guys he was going to bring in. Once again, "We're going in another direction." Now I think I know why Shakespeare said, "Beware the Ides of March."

Miami head coach Eric Spoelstra was one of the first people to call me after I was let go from the Knicks. We have been friends since my early days in the NBA, and he had mentioned on several occasions that he was a big fan of our offense in Phoenix. I joined the Heat in an unofficial capacity as his offensive advisor two weeks later.

The Heat's legendary former coach Pat Riley and team owner Micky Arison had established what was, in my opinion, the absolute best culture in the NBA. They were clear about their core values and held people accountable to them. That catalyzed the Heat to be consistently successful over many years. Every Heat fan knows that their leadership will always strive to build teams to do things the right way and win games. In 2008, Pat Riley decided to step down as head coach, and the Heat named assistant coach Erik Spoelstra as his successor. Spo has masterfully continued that culture that is still in place today.

The governor of the Knicks, Jim Dolan, and the entire Knicks organization does everything in a first class manner. They give their employees everything they need to be successful, and that was clear to me from day one. I will always cherish my time in New York. Growing up on Long Island as a Knicks fan, it was a surreal experience for me to coach for the Knicks in fabled Madison Square Garden. Add to the mix that I was working in front of some of the best basketball fans in the world, often including members of my own family. It was a very special time in my career, and I will always cherish those memories.

CULTURES MAY VARY

What people must understand is that all cultures are not the same. Just as coaches and teachers have different styles, quality cultures can have a range of different characteristics. All great cultures play off the strengths of their leaders and organizations. Just like individual coaches, teachers, and leaders can inspire and make people thirsty, cultures can differentiate themselves through the tremendously varied environments they create for growth. As I mentioned, the organizational cultures that stand out to me are San Antonio and Miami as well as the cultures I experienced working with Mike D'Antoni.

> All great cultures play off the strengths of their leaders and organizations.

Erik Spoelstra, Gregg Popovich, and Mike D'Antoni all have built and maintained top-level cultures, but you would never say that they are the same. I think if you ask great leaders what allows them to create their cultures, each would identify their main players (or employees and managers) as the reason why they succeeded. San Antonio had Tim Duncan and Manu Ginobili. The Miami Heat had Alonzo Mourning, who passed it down to Dwyane Wade and Udonis Haslem. In Phoenix, we had the highly experienced Steve Nash, who joined forces with a super talented young core. These players allowed their coaches to coach them in their own style. And all these leaders had different methods, which led to very different cultures, but they were all successful.

High standards are inherent in all quality cultures, but it's how you implement them that separates the cultures. For instance, with the Heat, they go to great lengths to not only talk about hard work but also show it to you. How do they do that? A player's body fat is taken as soon as they become a member of the Heat, and a shirtless picture is taken on the infamous iPad. In a short period of time, they will clearly see the benefits of their hard work.

In Mike D'Antoni's culture, that was not necessarily the case. He also had those high standards and expectations, but he did not emphasize them in the same way. Mike was actually somewhat easygoing—he was open-minded and trusted people to do their job as it was discussed. This allowed me, while charting offense, to keep showing different offensive possibilities. The players knew that all the work they did was geared toward winning. During our years in Phoenix, we would practice at a high level but in short bursts. We believed that our guys would practice so hard for a couple of reasons. First, they trusted us because we would not have a long, drawn-out practice simply for the sake of practicing. Second, we just had a great group of guys. Mike and I had many conversations about personnel, during which something became very clear: If you have really good guys on your team, strict rules are not necessary. If you have bad guys on your team, they would not follow the rules anyway. The more hard-core rules you have, the more issues you end up with. The absolute key was to bring in quality people as well as high-level players. I believe that all quality cultures can reflect that attribute.

We had an all-around great player in Phoenix named Bo Outlaw. He was absolutely dynamic defensively, and no one played harder than Bo. His only real weakness was that he struggled to shoot the ball from the perimeter. During my charting, one occurrence kept happening over and over, so it became quite noticeable to me. When the shot clock was running out, Bo would frequently have the ball on the perimeter because his defender would be sagging off him out there and he would be forced to shoot. The strange thing was that Bo usually knocked it in. This happened so much that I came up with a corny little saying: "When the shot clock's low, get it to Bo!" What happened in those instances was that Bo knew he had to shoot it, his team knew he had to shoot it, and so did all the fans, so Bo confidently let it fly, with zero doubt.

To me, playing in Mike's culture created the same mindset: zero doubt. Agents love to send their players to a team coached by Mike, because in most cases, they have career years. When Mike accepted the job to coach the Knicks, I was one of his first hires. Even though I was from New York, my friends in Phoenix would kid me about how cold the winters were going to be when I moved out there from Phoenix. My standard reply was always that Mike was my weather, because I knew every single day what the forecast for being in a successful working environment was going to be. One of the things I noticed about Mike was that every day on the practice court, he would walk around to each player to make sure that they were OK. Mike treated players as men who are able to give their opinions, and they feel safe doing so because of the culture.

Shawn Achor, author of *The Happiness Advantage*, points out that feeling good about what you are doing and where you are doing it brings higher-quality work and more success.[20] Feeling safe in an environment allows you to expand and to be unconcerned about other people's agendas. When a culture has one mission and one agenda—to be the best—that culture will thrive. When individual agendas are allowed to exist within a culture, it's like a cancer just waiting to fully expand and ultimately destroy that culture from the inside out.

A major attribute of each one of these three coaches is a high level of emotional intelligence. Leaders lead people, not things. As a leader, you have to care about those you are leading in order to continue to grow and evolve within that established culture.

> When a culture has one mission and one agenda—to be the best—that culture will thrive.

These three coaches are also the main broadcasting mechanisms for their cultures, but again, they all play that role in very different ways. It is important to remember that what you focus on grows. For example, in Miami, like all quality cultures, they reinforce their culture by being mindful of the teaching moment. From my personal experience, I know that Mike and Spo are masters at that. I have heard that Coach Popovich is as well.

For example, Udonis Haslem was a player for the Heat, but he hadn't gotten into a game for over two months. Even so, he came in every day, worked hard, stayed focused, and had a great attitude. Then, during a playoff game, he ended up having to play because of the

---

20   Shawn Achor, *The Happiness Advantage: How a Positive Brain Fuels Success in Work and Life* (New York: Currency, 2010).

injuries and foul trouble of other Heat players. He played very well but got only a couple of points and rebounds. Dwyane Wade played like his usual superstar self, and the Heat won the game. Coach Spoelstra still used Haslem's playing as a teachable moment. The first thing he talked about when he got in front of the team in the locker room was how Udonis had been coming in every day, working hard, and staying ready to play and how that helped the Heat get the big win.

Spo told me many times that if you combined the Heat's defensive culture with the offensive mindset and culture that we had in Phoenix, it would be amazing. That was exactly my mindset when I was given the opportunity to coach the Heat's G League team, the Sioux Falls Skyforce. We ended our season winning our division for the first time in the Heat's Skyforce history while being a top ten defensive team and having the league's best effective field goal percentage of 55 percent. My time with Spo was such a growing experience. I had the opportunity to learn from one of the best and to see firsthand what a tremendous culture the Heat had. I also realized how important culture is to any team. It is my hope that for all the Heat gave me, I was able to leave just a bit of our offensive mindset in Miami.

How you create a quality culture will be determined by your leadership. Is your group or team aligned with one goal, one mission? How does your leadership illustrate what is valued in your culture? Do they walk their own talk? Does your culture embrace growth and change? Are there mixed agendas, or is your group tightly consolidated around the same vision? These questions and more must be answered as you develop your quality culture.

THE HOTEL WAR ROOM

When I first went to Miami, we established my suite, room 214, in the Coconut Grove Ritz as our war room. Erik Spoelstra lived on the tenth floor in the residential section of the hotel, so it was extremely convenient. I was an unofficial offensive advisor to the head coach that first spring and became an official employee for the next two seasons, working directly alongside Spo. That was a special time, and I continued to learn from others about how to help people develop and improve. One side benefit was that the war room hosted visits from Spo's entire family and longtime friends during the playoffs. Due to the Heat's success, winning two World Championships and achieving a playoff series record of 11–1, there were many good times in room 214!

In 2014–2015, I was fortunate to be a part of the Heat training camp. That summer I was hired to be the head coach of the Heat's G League team, the Sioux Falls Skyforce, for the 2014–2015 season. I got to experience, up close, the power of the culture that Coach Riley established and that Coach Spoelstra has diligently and seamlessly continued.

I was able to learn so much just by being around Spo, whether that was from conversing with him, watching the decisions that he made, seeing how practices were run (the first two years on tape), or, most importantly, seeing how he was the voice that carried out Coach Riley and Micky Arison's vision. Spo modeled the Heat's core values. I was able to see how those levels of daily accountability directly related to the success and tight bond of an entire franchise. It was very clear to me that many players who were undervalued or had little success on other teams would thrive when they joined the Heat. It makes no difference whether you call it the *environment* or the *culture*, but it is a vital piece of the development process. It is no surprise to me that people who work with the Heat find it hard to leave. A key component of a strong culture is that everyone in it feels safe. Also, the stronger the culture, the faster the development. As I write this, I can clearly see the impact on undrafted and G League players Kendrick Nunn, Duncan Robinson, and Derrick Jones Jr.

What is the environment of your team, school, or workplace? Who are the main voices that guide your environment? What are the primary points consistently relayed to the players? These are powerful questions that will determine the direction of your team.

CHAPTER 9

INSTILL CONFIDENCE WITH SMALL VICTORIES

Confidence is the most important single factor in this game, and no matter how great your natural talent, there is only one way to obtain and sustain it: work.

—Jack Nicklaus

What is your skill level the first time you try to do something? What is your confidence level? I have been a basketball player and then a coach my entire life, so other winter sports were never an option. But as fate would have it, one year while I was coaching at the University of Florida, the NCAA Final Four was held in Denver. While there, I decided to head out to Vail to go skiing. One of my best friends in the world is Roger Maris Jr. (his dad was the Roger Maris who broke

Babe Ruth's home run record). Roger was an accomplished skier, and he loaned me all his gear, so I was all set without spending a fortune.

DON'T SKIP STEPS

I remember that all my ski-savvy friends agreed that the first time you try skiing, you should take a lesson to learn the basics. When I got to Vail, I immediately signed up for and headed to the bunny slope where the instruction took place. My confidence level as I took my first couple of steps was an absolute zero. With my skis on, I inched up to where the instructor stood and met my classmates. They were all five- or six-year-olds who were waiting with their parents. Talk about humbling. I sweated through the lessons as my extremely young fellow students blew past me. Once I learned the basics of how to turn and stop quickly, I made the decision to join all the advanced skiers on the real mountain. In my mind, it was a well-calculated gamble. Not smart!

Our instructor taught us the importance of mastering the basics first (the same thing I tell basketball players). He said that there were three levels of slopes: green for beginners (me), blue for intermediate, and black for expert. I jumped on the ski lift with all my gear solidly in place and gazed through my yellow goggles as I ascended the mountain on that clear, cold day. "Take it easy, get the basics down, and don't break anything" became my mantra. I jumped off at the first green trail sign I saw and started, very cautiously, down the hill. I peered at the trail, and this supposedly beginner run looked like jumping off a cliff. Yikes! I paused at the point of no return, and as I did, a teenage skier went speeding past. I yelled, "Yo, is this a green trail?"

My skiing counterpart quickly replied, "No, dude, this is the toughest blue on the mountain!"

Later I profoundly realized that when you look at a blue circle through yellow goggles, it looks green. That day I broke the record for the slowest time down that trail on my way to a treacherous ending. I did eventually make it to the bottom, right at the place where all seven trails on the mountain converge. I wiped out right there, and I really struggled to get up. What a moment as I awkwardly tried to stand up on icy snow with these long foreign objects on my feet while seven trails' worth of skiers whizzed by me at high speeds. As my short two-day trip went on, I got a bit better, but not much. I realized that I'd learned a little about skiing, but I'd learned a lot about learning.

Like the advice my friends gave me to take lessons and head to the bunny slope first, we should always start with basic, simple fundamentals as building blocks at the beginning of learning any skill. The Spurs mantra was to never skip steps. Stephen Covey would tell you that some things come before other things. For instance, with Kobe, after analyzing what I thought were the issues, I broke it down into small, specific pieces of his shot, starting less than one foot from the basket. I will not get into the minutiae of Kobe's shot, but I will tell you that my coach speak was constant. It usually included words and phrases like *beautiful, awesome, that was your best one yet today, concentrate, lock in,* or *that was amazing.* The keys are being present every step of that movement with the player, monitoring to see if it was correct, finding a word to emphasize how good the repetition was, and being constructive and empowering in every repetition that needs correction.

SUCCESS AS A TEACHER

So many successful teachers, managers, and coaches emphasize the importance of catching the other person doing something right. Why is that so important? In almost all these building blocks of development, the power of our mind is front and center. There's a phrase I will borrow from Joe Dispenza, who says that what's fired together is wired together. When you do something right, you throw in a mantra and then you finalize with an emphasizing positive comment. That whole process becomes part of the "wire" you want to create. As you continue to do quality rep after quality rep, you will build that steel cable, as I previously mentioned in working with Amar'e Stoudemire on his shot. Building that new steel cable, step by step, rep by rep, the correct way, is essential to the process. Constant positive feedback is also a necessity and is what gives real fuel to the process.

As you are teaching skills, remember that all students are different. The differences are found in many varieties. Take, for example, a young rookie who is drafted after just one year of college. He is extremely talented but may have established some bad habits. You should teach him one way, most likely using all the techniques to trigger and instill quality habits. Or, if you are lucky enough to work with Steve Nash, a player in the middle of his Hall of Fame, two-time MVP career, your preparation for the workout would be to see how to challenge him enough to push him further. With a player like Steve, the amount of talk would be much different, focusing on something very specific. He is probably also helping and coaching you to be a better coach. In most cases, the type and amount of coach speak would be totally different for the younger player with less skill and experience. When I think of this approach visually, I keep something like this in mind:

COACHING APPROACH PREFERRED	PLAYER SKILL LEVEL	PLAYER CONFIDENCE LEVEL
Asking	Skilled	Confident
Discussing		
Listening		
Modeling	Moderately skilled	Moderately confident
Showing		
Repeating	Unskilled	Unconfident
Telling		

For a great example of a veteran player trying to improve on a skill later in his career, I refer to Hall of Famer Shaquille O'Neal. In Phoenix, we made a late trade for him with Miami in the 2007–2008 season. To put things in perspective, the trade happened almost three-fourths of the way through the season. Shaq knew that he was coming to a playoff team and that he would continue to be a target to get fouled every game.

Because Shaq trusted me, and because I respected his work ethic, we were able to develop a strong relationship to quickly address his shooting. I have never worked with anyone so focused on improving his free-throw shots. The work we did centered on clearing his mind of doubt and instilling supreme confidence. We spent night after night simplifying and improving his stroke. What isn't mentioned enough is that Shaq could not bend his wrist back in a normal fashion because of a previous injury. This made it basically impossible for him to give the shot the proper amount of arc. Our goal was to simplify his shooting motion but also to give him a crazy amount of confidence when he stepped up to the line.

The amount of coach speak from me was significant and predominantly confidence-driven. The major challenge that Shaq and I faced was that it was so late in the season that we had very little normal practice time. I learned from my research that many coaches had worked with Shaq to improve his shooting, so he already had received several suggestions; the last thing he needed was a major overhaul. Plus, the absence of practice time meant that he would have to shoot free throws during the game while he was in the middle of improving his shot. This is not a good scenario for anyone trying to implement any kind of change. As a result, we kept the adjustments as small as possible.

During these games, if Shaq missed a free throw, he would always look over at me on the bench to see what I thought he did wrong. Invariably my only response during games was, "Just step up and knock it in." The worst thing you can do is to make a player think about the process of shooting during a game. It needs to be automatic and shot as if they are certain that it's going to go in. In competition, confidence and flow generally outperform analysis and nonflow perfect form. By the time he left the Suns, Shaq had won some games for us by knocking in his free throws. This is another testimony to the importance of the right mindset. Mike D'Antoni would leave Shaq in the game to further our staff's belief in his ability and to reward Shaq's determination to work hard and focus.

I can't mention Shaq's learning style without talking about his style in general. It was hilarious to see Shaq arrive at the arena. He drove a massive oversize tractor trailer truck cab with a crazy loud horn. He would blast that horn in the belly of the arena to see people's reactions. In those situations, I really saw the playful and humorous side of Shaq. It was an honor to coach him, and he was one of the game's most dominant and greatest players. Period.

We must always understand and plan to help a player establish the ideal mindset and to raise their confidence level. They must believe in and respond to what you are telling them in order to increase their confidence level. What type of praise and correction best works for your player, student, or coworker? It is imperative that you constantly analyze what is working with each person. You will need to understand what type of learner they are. Maybe they are a visual learner, so they need to see themselves achieving success. Or maybe they really respond to the way you praise their small advances. Those who have the greatest success will be the ones who take the time to understand the learning style of the person they are coaching.

This entire section was all about relationships. If, as I believe, relationships are the cornerstone of the coach/player development process, then the actual plan is the road map—and that's what we'll tackle next.

> Those who have the greatest success will be the ones who take the time to understand the learning style of the person they are coaching.

SECTION 3: THE PLAN

LIFE ILLUSTRATES

Every moment of every single day, we tell the world who we are. Do we walk through our day focused on solutions, or are we a magnet to all the obstacles or negative things that are happening in the world? Are we a person of integrity, where our actions always follow our words, or do we tell people things knowing that it really doesn't matter what you say before you move on to the next situation? Do we look to forgive freely, knowing that we may be coming from a place of incorrect judgment, and even if justified, do we want that anger and negativity inside us, understanding that it is like a poison that affects the way we view the world in such a negative way? Do we have a moral compass, or are we a person who constantly seeks pleasures regardless of social or family cost? Are we sincere and helpful to *all* people or just to those who are able to help us in some way? Are we hard workers, or do we simply choose to work hard when in the focus of the world? Are we someone who takes pride in everything we do, striving to give more than expected, or do we do just enough to say that the job is done? Do we continually seek to grow and become the best possible versions of ourselves in all areas of our life, or do we simply float through life with a fixed interpretation of our ever-changing world? Are we compassionate and empathetic to all people, and do we look to help whenever it is possible, or are we self-absorbed in our own world? Are we humble in moments of success, or are we fixated and boast of current and past accomplishments? Are we living in the moment, or do we constantly spend our time reliving our past struggles and/or successes, or are we dreaming about some future world, unaware of this fleeting, invaluable present moment? Do we choose to live with a passion for life, or do we allow life's happenings to rob us from experiencing all its amazing wonders? Do we choose to live with a deep sense of gratitude, or is our focus on all the countless things that we don't have or the things that aren't happening for us? Do we understand that we own the key to our entire world and that it is simply through our moment-by-moment focus that we can make our lives a masterful work of art?

—Phil Weber

CHAPTER 10

EVALUATE THE PLAYER/ EMPLOYEE

The best evaluation I can make of a player is to look in his eyes and see how scared they are.

—Michael Jordan

The number one trait I evaluate in any player is their thirst to get better. Not every player has the physical ability and the talent to reach the highest levels. But to maximize their gifts, they must demonstrate that growth mindset, which indicates that they will do whatever it takes. They will thrive through the boredom, pain, and frustration to get better. The biggest question is this: Does the talent chase the thirst, or does the thirst chase the talent? When you have high levels of both, special things happen.

There are many steps involved in constructing a building, and one of the first is to hire an architect to create a blueprint based on what you want the finished product to be. The architect will need to visit the site and gather information in order to understand how the plan should go and how the building should fit in with the location. The architect would include in their vision all the things that are necessary for ideal functionality as well as what the building will look like when completed.

WORK FROM THE GROUND UP

The same concept applies when you are starting the process of coaching or teaching. It is important to fully understand where your journey of development is starting with your player and where you want to end up. Like an architect, you have to assess the player and the conditions by asking yourself questions like the following:

- At what level are we starting?

- What trust and respect level do I have with this player?

- What strengths and weaknesses does this player have? Are they a naturally hard worker, or will they need to be pushed? Are they a fast learner?

- How will I push the player?

- Are there important emotional triggers I can use to positively motivate the player?

- If I have options, what type of environment will be best?

- What will be the best way to instill a growth mindset?

- How confident is the player?

- Will I need to boost the player up or create situations to humble them, skills-wise, in order to get their full attention?

- How detailed can I get when breaking down the drills or video?

Before I get into specific plans for players, I should mention that, as a coach, my approach is to always work with players to improve in all skills. Regardless of what specific weaknesses a player is working to improve, overfocusing comes at the risk of ignoring versatility. So often players are pigeonholed. "He is a shooting guard. This guy is a five. That other guy is a small forward." It was never my plan to put a player into a box or to create false and limiting beliefs about what type of player they could become. My goal for every plan is to improve in all aspects of the game and to continually push the player to become highly efficient in all areas. However, I also believe in maximizing God-given talents in order to reach a player's full potential.

> Regardless of what specific weaknesses a player is working to improve, overfocusing comes at the risk of ignoring versatility.

START WITH STRENGTHS

There has been a major effort in the business world to focus on strengths rather than on weaknesses. In their book *Now, Discover Your Strengths*, Marcus Buckingham and Don Clifton emphasize the need to help people identify their unique strengths and understand that they can have more impact doing those things more and better than trying to improve on the things they don't do well.[21] Their theory is that some weaknesses cannot be forced into submission and

---

21 Marcus Buckingham and Donald O. Clifton, *Now, Discover Your Strengths* (New York: Free Press, 2001).

turned into a strength. For some of those weaknesses, it is better to create a way to manage around them. In other words, create a work-around. In chapter 3, I mentioned the work I did with Boris Diaw, and he is a great example of this concept. Boris was gifted in so many areas of his game, but one weakness we worked on (but did not get overly worked up about) was his ability to use his left hand. Boris was so good at working around it by going to his right that it did not present a problem for him. Sometimes by emphasizing strengths and zeroing in on improving one weakness, you can work around other weaknesses.

BE FLEXIBLE WITH YOUR EVALUATION

Evaluating players is always a process. You never want to be too quick to judge, and you have to be open to your evaluation evolving as the process continues. A great example of this was when I worked with Danilo Gallinari in his rookie year with the Knicks. We drafted Gallo in 2008, and from my initial evaluation, I had him slotted in as a skilled forward. A multifaceted player who could do it all, Gallo was six foot ten and somewhat slight of build, but we could see that he had a great frame. He could handle pick and rolls, which would eventually be a real differentiator for what the NBA used to call a *power forward*. Gallo was a great shooter and pretty quick, although that was an area that would improve as he continued to physically mature. We watched a lot of video of Gallo and could tell that he was a smart player. We felt that Gallo could be a special player in the NBA.

As Gallo's rookie season began and the real evaluation process started, we had a plan in place for his development. But later in his rookie season, he raised his ceiling significantly in my eyes. One day, toward the end of a workout, Gallo was shooting three-pointers from five different spots around the arc. In one spot, Gallo knocked in ten in a row shooting with his normal right hand, then he put the ball in his left hand and knocked in another ten in a row with perfect shooting form. How crazy is that?

Still amazed at what I had just witnessed, I asked Gallo as we were walking off the court why it was that he was so good with his left hand. He told me that as a kid growing up in Italy, he was naturally a left-hander. Around age eight, he was watching some tapes of his father's games with his dad, who was a pro in Italy and a teammate of Mike D'Antoni's. Gallo asked his dad, "Why are all the players shooting with their right hand?" His dad didn't know. Gallo said that from that day on, he worked to become a right-handed player, just like all the pros. I had to revisit my evaluation of Gallo and raise his developmental blueprint as a result of his ambidextrous ability. As history will show, Gallo is and will be remembered as a tremendous NBA player.

PLAYERS BRING UNIQUE STRENGTHS

The 1999–2000 season was my first in Phoenix, and that year the Suns had landed NBA veteran Rodney Rogers. He was a strong, talented forward and first-round draft pick from Wake Forest University. For his size, he already had many of the necessary skills for an NBA forward and then some. One of the things I repeat often is that coaching is emphasizing. The things we emphasized with Rodney were his footwork to get his shot on the perimeter, his post-up moves, and locking in his three-point range. Due to Rodney's physical size and gifts, he was a nightmare for defenders. He could punish a smaller player if he took him down in the post, and he had the skills that allowed him to be efficient from the perimeter if he had a quickness advantage. In our plan, we would emphasize the footwork to free up perimeter shots and his three-pointers, in addition to working on skills for all positions. Again, it was always my belief never to pigeon-hole a player with only specific positional drills. We would work on everything but choose certain skills to emphasize.

Rodney and I would work out after practice, and we also had a twenty-minute routine before every game. After one pregame workout, I had a memorable moment when Hall of Fame coach Dr. Jack Ramsey, who was one of the broadcasters doing color commenting for our game, sat by himself watching Rodney's and my pregame session. Afterward, he took me aside and told me how he loved the footwork drills we used and how perfect that routine was to take a player through before a game. When you hear something like that from a person with such a deep knowledge of the sport, it reinforces your belief that you're headed in the right direction.

As a result of a combination of factors, Rodney had a great season. His personal ethic of hard work, plus Scott Skiles's offensive scheme, positioned Rodney to break out. In addition, he was playing on a team led by Hall of Fame point guard Jason Kidd, Rex Chapman, and Tom Gugliotta. Rodney had a great season and earned the NBA's Sixth Man of the Year Award. All his efficiency numbers went up that year, including shooting 48 percent from the field and 43 percent from three-point range. Rodney was a big reason we won fifty-three games and beat San Antonio in the first round of the playoffs.

EACH BLUEPRINT IS UNIQUE

To illustrate how different a plan can be, during the 2003 draft process, we brought in Leandro Barbosa for a workout. Leandro is a six-foot-four guard from Brazil. He had just worked out in Seattle, and when he arrived in Phoenix, his agent said that Leandro was injured and wouldn't be able to train. We all felt that Seattle must have made a promise to take him in the draft. We must have been wrong, because when we asked him to at least shoot around, he obliged. And did he shoot! He absolutely lit it up by making eleven three-point shots in a row from the left corner and then the left forty-five-degree mark. He sank forty-three out of fifty and made it look easy.

During the 2003 draft, the Suns made a trade with San Antonio to get a protected first pick, and we selected Leandro Barbosa with the twenty-eighth pick of the first round. Leandro looked fast on the grainy black-and-white videotape that was passed around the NBA, but when we got him to Phoenix, we quickly learned that was an absolute under-statement. Leandro became known as the Brazilian Blur.

After the NBA draft concluded, the teams headed to their summer leagues. I was to be the head coach of the Suns' summer league team in Salt Lake City and LA that summer. Because Leandro had come directly to us from Brazil and had never played in the US, his English wasn't very good at the beginning. It was important to me to connect with him and to integrate him into the team as soon as possible. To make communication easier and to indoctrinate him into some of the US NBA culture, I took Leandro aside when we got to Salt Lake City. I tapped him with my right hand and said, "I now dub thee LB!" He greeted that announcement with his always-big LB smile.

In addition to his six-foot-four height, LB had a six-foot-ten wingspan. He was wiry, strong, quick, and extremely fast. As I mentioned earlier, from his workout we knew that he could flat-out shoot from three. He had an unusual form on his perimeter shot, but I would never try to change a player's technique just to make it look conventional. Our blueprint with Leandro was to stay basic to start with. We set three points of emphasis: finishing around the basket, improving his midrange jump shots, and maximizing the effect of his incredible speed so that we could leverage one of his greatest strengths.

LB's shot from three-point range was amazing. It was like the ball was on a rope as it went toward the basket. A drawback to his form was that the arc was flatter than normal, and his shot was more of a line drive. The lack of arc really didn't impact his three-point shooting due to the distance and angle that the ball traveled. However, when LB would penetrate the lane, defenders were closer, and his midrange shots needed a higher release point and more arc. That would allow his ball to arrive softer at the rim. To work on finishing near the rim, we helped him anticipate a seven-footer coming over to block his shot as well as all the different angles that could present themselves. I used a taped-up hockey stick that I brought from LA, which I called the *equalizer,* to mimic a big center coming over to block LB's layups.

The following year we were fortunate to sign Hall of Fame point guard Steve Nash. By watching and learning from Steve, both LB and I were able to expand the menu of LB's finishes. Steve opened my eyes to so many things, but he was the absolute master of finishing. LB and I started to incorporate finishes that Steve used into LB's workouts. NBA players are much better these days at finishing. It was much less common before Steve Nash. He was a transformative player.

One of the major decisions I made early on with LB's development plan was in regard to his ball handling. We worked on all the individual dribble moves every day, but we seriously emphasized the high crossover. To me, the high crossover enabled LB to maximize his amazing speed. Stopping and then starting again, using deception (which is a major component of basketball IQ), was going to be a huge point of emphasis for LB's plan. I do not want to get too technical in this book on specific skills and how to teach them, but knowing how to break them down and sequentially build them up creates the primary building blocks for all skills. Understanding this is a necessity for every coach.

LB's development plan was to study and learn the Suns' team and its individual defensive fundamentals, emphasize midrange shots with increased arc, improve his variety of finishes, and make his high crossover one of the best offensive weapons in the NBA. Due to LB's hard work and his improving English, he quickly became an integral part of the team. Having Steve Nash as a model for the point guard position accelerated LB's development. In 2005–2006, after two years of gradually expanding LB's development plan and having a full year under his belt playing with Steve Nash, another major component in LB's development fell into place—the leadership of Coach Dan D'Antoni.

EVOLVE THE ASSESSMENT TO FIT THE TEAM

That year the Suns built up a record of 62–20 and ultimately a loss in the Western Conference Finals. As I mentioned earlier, we lost Joe Johnson, a major contributor to our success in the previous 2004–2005 season. After losing Joe, we gained Boris Diaw. Then, one week into training camp during the 2005–2006 season, we received some bad news. Amar'e Stoudemire would need microfracture surgery and would miss the whole season. How could that happen? It was now time to regroup and find a way to play without our All-Star center.

ROTATING RESOURCES

The coaching staff decided that I would work with Boris, who was super talented but who had underachieved in Atlanta. The responsibility for continuing to develop LB would go to Dan D'Antoni, Mike D'Antoni's older brother, who had joined our staff during that 2005–2006 season. Those decisions turned out to be excellent all around. Dan established a strong bond with LB, and that, combined with all the previous components mentioned in LB's plan, catapulted him to win the NBA's Sixth Man of the Year Award. I learned a tremendous lesson that season—the relationship between the player and the coach is vital and foundational. One of the things Dan would do before each game was to write a letter to LB outlining the things that he felt the player should focus on during that particular game. That is something I would always tell players, but I never wrote it down in letter form. Many times, at the end of the letter, Dan would tell LB that he loved him. How powerful is that? LB was living so far away from his home country and was having to learn the English language, but now his coach was telling him almost daily that he loved him. Over the hundreds of hours of working with LB the previous two seasons, I'd made it my goal to show LB that I did love him by my preparation and in any other way that I could. But at the time, I didn't say it often, if at all. Nowadays, whenever I have an opportunity to connect with LB, I always say it, and many times he beats me to the punch. What a tremendous illustration of caring about the player you're working with, and it goes a long way toward bolstering a player's self-esteem, which I will address later in the book.

The 2005–2006 season was special for all of us. The awards are, of course, given at the end of the season. But in hindsight, I thought about our practices and games when I would look out on the court and see a team that included the NBA's Most Improved Player (Boris

Diaw), the NBA's Sixth Man of the Year (LB), and the NBA's Most Valuable Player (Steve Nash). All three of those awards are league awards selected from over four hundred NBA players. Without our All-Star center, we won fifty-four games and made it to the Western Conference Finals. In game one of the finals, we lost Raja Bell, our starting two-guard who was a 40 percent three-point shooter and one of our best perimeter defenders, to a calf injury. Dallas took advantage and won the hard-fought series.

CHAPTER 11

CREATE THE PLAN

Create a definite plan for carrying out your desire and begin at once, whether you are ready or not, to put this plan into action.

—Napoleon Hill

Creating a plan gives action to the vision that you and the player have built. Coaching is all about emphasizing, so there will be specific focus points that you will incorporate into the plan. All this is done with the knowledge that, because all players are different, there isn't one plan that fits everyone.

FUNDAMENTALS FIRST

At the foundation of any development plan are the basic fundamentals. It's analyzing the vision that takes your plan in different directions. As a coach, you always want to develop the widest foundation to build on. There are usually many variables that impact the plan, including age, physical condition, skill level, experience, athleticism, maturity level, basketball IQ, and initial level of desire. The other variable is the player's role on the team.

These factors also affect the quantity and kind of input a player will contribute to the plan. A player just embarking on their career will need to be more open to getting direction and structure from coaches. With a veteran player, it becomes more of a discussion about what they've experienced, where they think we need to emphasize our efforts, and where they think it is best to build from. Again, all players are different and bring completely unique attributes, so you need to consider their specific levels. As you discuss the plan with your player, place the emphasis on real improvement while explaining that the path will predictably go through boredom, pain, and sometimes long plateaus with little improvement before a major jump happens.

THE IMPORTANCE OF CHALLENGE AND SUPPORT

The plan should focus on experience and skill level as the initial main components. The reason for this is that you want to develop a plan that reinforces existing skills as a starting place to build the all-important player confidence. The plan should be easy enough to make them feel good about the skills they bring but should challenge them to get to the next level. I like to use the metaphor of rock climbing. A player will be climbing the mountain at their own pace, reaching for one rock at a time and only stretching for that next rock once they feel secure in their present footing. They gain confidence with each step as they reach up and grab a rock just a little bit higher. Once they have it and feel safe, they can reach up for the next rock. The process of moving successfully up to the next level builds more confidence. The workouts should be challenging but not so hard as to cause serious frustration to seep in.

Physical condition is an obvious part of developing your plan. If a player is out of shape, it's usually very visible. Getting a player into shape will always be a foundational building block. Unfortunately, there have been too many stories of NBA players who, due to their weight and lack of conditioning, had much shorter and less profitable careers. A player's condition is squarely in their circle of influence. John Wooden would always emphasize that he worked with players for only a couple of hours a day, so he counted on them to pay attention to their conditioning away from practice as well. When a skilled player is out of condition, it has been my experience that they look for opportunities to coast. Players in supreme shape look to excel.

The conditioning aspect of the plan must be included in all the drills you create. Anyone can make a workout hard by telling players to get on the line and having them run back-and-forth line drills (commonly called *suicides* by basketball players) until they throw up. That takes zero skill from the coach. The best plan is one with focused intensity that takes into account each player's skills and needs while including the necessary elements of conditioning.

In basketball, as in most sports, people tend to overuse the generic word *athleticism*. When creating a plan for a specific player, you break athleticism down into its component parts to be considered in the vision you have for that particular player. All these factors are interrelated in the core vision. For example, consider the plans for two players on our 2004–2005 Phoenix Suns team, Steve Nash and Leandro Barbosa. They were both excellent point guards but were at very different places in their careers and had different levels of skill, experience, and basketball IQ. What they had in common was a serious desire to be the best. Two players, same position, same team, same goal, but different plans for development.

METRICS MATTER

What are the foundational elements to take into consideration in what you're teaching? Have you broken them down and identified which ones are most important in order to emphasize them in your plan?

More than fifty years ago, Peter Drucker, an author and business guru, famously said, "What gets measured gets managed."[22] Analytics must be a part of any plan to determine how much progress the player is making relative to the skill they're developing. For example, if you are looking to improve your three-point shooting, you need to establish your current baseline first before you quantify your goal for improvement. That's a very simple example. These days, analytics are a part of every sport, and teams are investing more and more into tracking and interpreting these data. To create deeper analytics and to show how we might consider three-point effectiveness, we need to

> Analytics must be a part of any plan to determine how much progress the player is making relative to the skill they're developing.

---

22   Peter F. Drucker, *The Practice of Management* (New York: Harper Business, 1954).

take it a step further by working on threes because of spacing and the dynamics on the court. And because you make two out of four threes, that's six points. You make two out of four twos, that's only four points. The effective field goal percentage is one of the main things you pay attention to from an analytics perspective.

Another example of the effect of analytics is the extent to which centers shoot from three-point range. When I first got into the league, there were only a handful of centers who would practice three-point shots. Today, most centers are shooting threes in warm-ups and in practice. Analytics has changed the game. It's changed emphasis, and as a result, you must adjust your plan.

ANALYTICS IN DEVELOPMENT

Analytics as we know it today was not a hot topic when I first broke into the league in 1999. Our video coordinator for the Phoenix Suns was a brilliant guy named Garrick Barr. He and his up-and-coming assistant, David Griffin, put together and weighed statistics in relationship to winning. To my knowledge, it was the first attempt to weigh a player's statistics in relation to winning as a way to evaluate a player's effectiveness. They called it a *player's BBIQ*. The NBA now uses something called *player efficiency rating*, or PER, which is the modern-day version of Garrick's BBIQ and is one approach to summarizing a player's impact with one number. Garrick would eventually leave the Suns to start a super successful company called Synergy Sports Technology, which provides analytics to NBA teams and essentially all college and pro teams around the globe. David Griffin climbed the NBA front office ladder, including a stint as the GM of the Cleveland Cavaliers when they won the NBA championship. He is currently the executive vice president of the New Orleans Pelicans.

Nowadays analytics are an essential tool to measure where a player is as well as which aspects of skill development should be a point of emphasis in relationship to their performance.

As an aside, we were highly criticized in Phoenix for taking so many three-point shots in 2004–2005. Pundits said that the Suns will live with the three or they'll die with the three. When you look at the NBA today, it's almost comical how few threes we were taking then and how many, on average, teams take now. We just wish we'd had a stronger conviction and built our team accordingly.

When I was coaching with the Knicks, Kenny Atkinson joined our staff as an assistant coach. This is a great small-world story. Growing up, Kenny's house was right around the corner from mine. Kenny is one of eight boys, and they all were athletes. His older brother Brian and I were in the same class and were good friends. Between the Atkinson boys and the rest of the neighborhood kids, I spent countless hours playing every sport in Kenny's yard. During our time together with the Knicks, I came to appreciate Kenny's acute awareness of the impact of statistics on efficiency. His playing background in Europe, along with his experience as a player development coach in Houston under GM Daryl Morey, influenced how he viewed the game. In turn, I learned a lot from my discussions with Kenny, and those conversations only deepened my belief in the importance of using performance-based analytics. Students get grades, salespeople have quotas, and managers have different metrics for effectiveness. Analytics are here to stay. The more efficient the data, the more detailed you can be on specific development tasks for each player and how it relates to performance. The constant challenge will always be how to get better data and how best to maximize that data to increase your team's efficiency.

CHAPTER 12

ESTABLISH THE STANDARDS

We are what we repeatedly do. Excellence, then, is not an act, but a habit.

—Aristotle

Establishing standards is an all-inclusive task. To maximize every skill session, you must have standards in place for mindset, intensity level, and language for each individual drill. Will you allow a workout to happen if the player is not fully engaged? As Jocko Willink states in his book *Extreme Ownership*, it's not what you preach that establishes you as a leader; it's what you tolerate that does.[23]

---

23 Jocko Willink and Leif Babin, *Extreme Ownership: How US Navy SEALs Lead and Win* (New York: St. Martin's Press, 2015).

KEEP STANDARDS HIGH

One summer when I was coaching with the Knicks, Al Harrington asked if I would work him out on Sunday. I obliged, of course. Any player request to work extra always gets an automatic and emphatic yes from me. Al and I met up at the Knicks training facility, and I was ready to go. Just me, a player who wants to get better, and a basketball court. In my mind, it doesn't get any better than that.

Al and I both warmed up and prepared ourselves for the workout. We got started and moved quickly into some difficult drills that required a fair degree of intensity. Five minutes into that portion of the workout, it became apparent to me that Al had been expecting a low-key, maintenance-type workout. I stopped and asked him, "Al, on a scale of one to ten, where is your intensity level right now? Because I know how gifted you are, and I've seen how hard you've worked in the past, and you are not even close to that same Al Harrington I have seen." Al didn't say a word. He just sprinted over to where we were running the last drill and proceeded to train harder than I've ever seen him work.

I was in my office the following morning when the Knicks' trainer came in and asked me, "What did you do to Al yesterday?"

"What do you mean?" I responded, surprised.

The trainer said, "He came in here calling you a beast!"

After thinking long and hard about that, and comparing it to other experiences I had working out with players, I have come to realize three things:

- A coach's main job is to establish and monitor standards.

- We all have a conscience and know how hard we are working.

- Asking the player the right question can prompt them to motivate themselves more than getting on their backs does. I don't understand those coaches who yell, scream, and berate players in the hope of creating a positive growth response.

Never miss an opportunity to teach and reinforce a message. If you pay attention to a player's words and body language and you don't feel that they're empowering, it is your duty to call that player out on it. Words such as *can't*, *tired*, and *impossible* must be struck from a player's vocabulary. When a player

> A coach's main job is to establish and monitor standards.

drops their eyes after a missed shot or shakes their head in frustration, a coach should use this as a teachable moment.

Every player is at a different point of skill development; therefore, the standards for each will likely be different. A good-shooting veteran player coming off a pick and roll to take a three-point shot would expect to make a higher percentage than a rookie who hasn't perfected their stroke and that skill yet.

Standards in skill workouts can be tricky. If the player is an undeveloped shooter and you make the individual standards too high, frustration and too much negative feedback may creep in. If the standards are too low, then the player is not challenged. It is for this very reason that the coach must be in sync with the player they are working with. You want to make the goal attainable but challenging and then incrementally improve until you stop and take a look back to see just how far you have come. This process can have a serious impact on the amount of confidence a player gets organically.

EFFORT BEYOND BASKETBALL

A golden nugget of life I use from Zen Buddhism is this: "How you do anything, is how you do everything." When I make my bed in the morning, it has to be perfect. When I used to cut lawns, it was imperative that I lined up the wheels of the lawn mower every trip up and down so that the rows looked totally uniform when I finished. Those two things are just personal standards that were instilled in me by my parents and that I have never forgotten. The standards that we set for ourselves as coaches, teachers, and anyone in a managerial position will dictate the results that we ultimately achieve. In my mind, there is no question about it.

When I was the head coach for the Miami Heat's G League team, the Sioux Falls Skyforce, it was up to me to establish the standards that I accepted in practice and in games. I had a situation where a player was simply going through the motions and not bringing the same focus and intensity that his teammates were. After pointing this out to him and asking him for more focus and intensity, he didn't step up. Unfortunately, this was two days before a playoff game. I simply asked him to stop practicing, essentially kicking him off the court. It was the second time that season that he had forced my hand and the second time that I had kicked him out. Unfortunately for him, this time we were not at our own practice facility. And because it was the G League, he couldn't leave and go home. He had to sit and watch the team practice. The intensity shown by everyone else practicing that day reached an even higher level, which is always the case when you remove the weakest commitment link.

Earlier in the book, I highlighted the intensity of Kobe Bryant's workouts. The standards that he set for himself propelled him to greatness. Standards are set by each individual separately, but it is also the coach's role to elevate the intensity and to focus each and every workout or film session. Raising the standards of what you accept from them as their coach will always create more focus and intensity.

THE EFFECT OF STANDARDS

When discussions turn to judging the truly great players in the NBA, rightly or wrongly they are compared by the number of titles they won. Bill Russell has eleven rings, Michael Jordan has six, and Kobe Bryant had five. That is the pecking order in the NBA. If you venture down to the college ranks and look at the coaches, John Wooden, who is considered by many (myself included) to be the best basketball coach at any level, won ten NCAA titles with the UCLA Bruins. Mike Krzyzewski of Duke has five NCAA championships, and so on. Players from any of those teams will often talk about the standards set by those coaches. Standards set for a basketball team, a group's culture, or an organization are like an invisible magnet that should be pulling the group members to collectively work harder and more effectively to reach common goals.

Establishing high standards creates a common mindset among and between the players you are working with. Those standards become a critical route toward creating your plan. The standards that you must establish immediately include things like punctuality, mutual manners, respect, levels of focus, and intensity.

When I think of standards and the effect that they have on a culture, I often think of the brave men and women in our armed forces. Their code of conduct includes standards that are established and ingrained into each and every person. Those standards affect every aspect of their lives, from what they wear to how they speak. When a player, team, or organization has high standards, those standards immediately translate into high expectations, which yields more efficient execution every time.

The Blue Angels is a group of sixteen US Navy and Marine Corps jet pilots, and I have always marveled at their execution. As a team, they perform amazing shows of execution and togetherness. Imagine what is required for a group of jets flying synergistically together at speeds as fast as seven hundred miles per hour, totally in sync and sometimes as close to each other as eighteen inches. Think about that! One maneuver a second too slow or too fast could mean a devastating crash. The standards you must meet just to get into this special group are staggering, but once you're in, the standards in their practices and mental preparedness are beyond what most of us can even comprehend.

It is common practice during the NBA free agency period for players to speak to potential teams before they sign, and many times they visit the prospective team as well. When players meet with Miami Heat head coach Erik Spoelstra, he will invariably tell them, "We are going to push you harder than you've ever been pushed before, so we may not be the right team for you." (This approach was passed down over the years from former Heat coach Pat Riley.) What do you think that statement does to the prospective player? Most likely it immediately conjures an image of situations of mental and physical fatigue, along with a certain unknown. It is my guess that most of those players make up their minds immediately. Those with a growth mindset and a desire to constantly improve are all in for the challenge. Those with a fixed mindset will probably think, *Hey, I don't need that. I can get similar money without that level of commitment,* and they will sign to play elsewhere.

Have you ever questioned yourself about how you can raise your standards? Because if you did, I bet you would come up with a couple of ideas immediately. We are the culmination of our thoughts. If you ask yourself empowering questions, you will receive empowering answers. Unfortunately, the opposite is also true. Examining the questions you ask yourself relative to standards is vital. Remember this Buddhist saying: "What we are today comes from our thoughts of yesterday, and present thoughts build our life of tomorrow."

CHAPTER 13

REINFORCE THE VISION

You've got to think about big things while you're doing small things, so that all the small things go in the right direction.

—Alvin Toffler

This chapter is about developing a kind of shorthand. And, true to the subject, it is also short. The idea is that once a player has a clear vision of where they want to go, and you have created a plan to get them there, the process doesn't switch to autopilot. It requires some kind of reminder for the player about that original vision and a simple way to keep it out in front of them.

GREEN AND CLEAN

In his landmark book *The 7 Habits of Highly Effective People*, Stephen Covey describes his efforts to help his young son take responsibility for keeping up with the maintenance of their neglected lawn.[24] Their grass is yellowing and patchy, and trash is strewn around here and there. He walks his son over to the edge of his neighbor's yard and says, "Look at that, green and clean. That's what we want our yard to look like." He talks to his son and asks him how he might plan to do it. They discuss picking up trash and setting out the sprinkler, but he lets his son create the actual plan. Many days later, Covey comes home from work to find his son across the street, playing football with his friends. He calls his son over and asks him how the yard work is going, and his son tells him it is going fine. "Is it green and clean?" His son looks around and has to admit that it isn't. Covey goes on to describe how they work through the summer, with his son in charge of the lawn. *Green and clean* is the shorthand they used to reinforce their vision of what they wanted the yard to be.

The same approach applies to players. They require subtle and constant reminders to reinforce where you are going. "You're on the right track," or "That's not where we want to go." "You're getting there, you're getting there. That was a big step today. You're getting there. You're getting closer." Another Covey metaphor I like is that an airplane on a journey from Airport A to Airport B is actually flying off track about 90 percent of the time. Radar provides real-time, quick corrections as feedback to keep it moving toward its destination, and you somehow arrive on time.

A big vision keeps players motivated and locked in. You want to let them know why you're working so hard, because sometimes in the

---

24   Covey, *The 7 Habits of Highly Effective People*.

boredom, frustration, and pain, it's the carrot that you hold out there. "Don't you remember? This is where we're trying to go." They can't get to where they are going with less effort than that. They've got to place maximum effort and maximum focus on the right things. For the coach, it's more art than science. You sense that their path is not one of high intensity or

> A big vision keeps players motivated and locked in.

high focus, and you don't want to overuse your cues because then they'll tune you out. You try to limit it to whenever you need to potentially snap them back. "Hey, why are we doing this? I believe in you. I believe that you can get there, but this effort's not going to do it." You use it only when you see that you have to. Imagine if Stephen Covey had used "green and clean" in every conversation he had with his son about any subject. It would quickly have lost its original meaning and influence.

THE PICTURE TELLS A STORY

Sometimes reinforcement for the player's vision comes from another source entirely. Earlier in the book, I mentioned working with Amar'e Stoudemire on his shot by creating a vision and a mantra. His vison was to have superior shooting form, and we created a mantra to seal the steps in his mind: "Jump up, take a picture, follow through. Jump up, take a picture, follow through." Amar'e's hard work was paying off, he was shooting well, and the Suns were on fire with a 31–4 record. We were playing in Indianapolis, and every morning the hotel gave out copies of *USA Today*. I smiled when I saw the photo on the cover of the sports section. When I got on the team bus to ride over to the game, Amar'e was already in his seat in the back. I walked on and held up the newspaper, because that cover photo was a close-up of Amar'e going up for a beautiful, perfect-form jumper. Jump up, take a picture, follow through. Not exactly divine intervention, but definitely a nice reinforcement of Amar'e's mantra and vision for developing his jump shot in order to help the team win.

Through repetition, small midcourse corrections, sparing feedback, and hard work, you can help a player reinforce their vision. As Alabama football coach Nick Saban says, you don't practice until you get it right; you practice until you can't get it wrong.

CHAPTER 14

CONSTANTLY INSTILL CONFIDENCE

For me, it's always been about preparation, and the more prepared I can be each week, the less pressure I feel and the more confident I am.

—Aaron Rodgers

Confidence comes from preparing for and then achieving the desired results. As a coach, I want the development plan for the player to produce results in a tangible way. There is an important distinction to be made here, and that is the difference between confidence and self-confidence. They might seem to be the same thing at first glance, yet there are slight but important distinctions.

CONFIDENCE

Confidence comes from the Latin word for "to trust," and it is developed by practice, knowledge, and mastery. The more experience and success you have with something, the more confident you are about being able to accomplish it. Confidence tends to apply to a specific skill or task. Let me offer a basketball example. I used this as part of my plan when working with players. Amar'e and Boris knew only too well that at the end of every workout they would need to knock in ten in a row from each

> The more experience and success you have with something, the more confident you are about being able to accomplish it.

elbow (the place where the lines meet at the free-throw line) before they got to stop for the day. The reason was that we planned to run a lot of offense through both of them at the elbow. If they were so accustomed to making ten in a row when they got the ball there, and if the defense was not covering them closely, they would have high confidence to just knock in that shot. By comparison, if Amar'e had the ball in the backcourt and was being heavily guarded by a smaller, quicker defender, I do not believe that he would feel overly confident in dribbling against that pressure. We can all think of examples of this in our own lives. I am confident in my ability to help players develop. I am confident in my ability to speak in front of a group. I am not confident in my chances at an Olympic medal in downhill skiing, for reasons that I painfully described earlier in the book.

SELF-CONFIDENCE

By comparison, self-confidence is a broader belief in your ability to succeed at things in general, specifically new challenges or situations that you have not faced in the past. It is about trusting your ability to take on something new. For example, even though I have never given a talk to a room full of one hundred kindergarten teachers, I have the self-confidence that I could do it. I have essential skills that I can call on, such as putting myself in others' shoes and considering their perspective; I have an ample supply of stories; I have (what I would like to think is) a self-deprecating sense of humor; and I bring a certain level of energy to a presentation. Does that sound boastful? Maybe, maybe not. It's just that I have self-confidence built on that foundation.

SELF-ESTEEM

Then we introduce the idea of self-esteem, which is something altogether different. Self-esteem isn't about trust in ourselves. The word *esteem* comes from the Latin for "to value," and it is about how we consider our worth. It is possible to have high self-confidence and low self-esteem. One doesn't always come with the other. There are plenty of examples of that in the sports and celebrity worlds, where the person appears invincible when performing, but their self-worth seems to be tied up in their need for status recognition or other things. I don't want to play amateur psychologist here, but it is critical for me, as a coach, to be realistic about what I can do to help someone in this part of their development and to understand what my limitations are.

When I am working with a player, I am clear that my job is to help build their confidence. I can have a direct impact by helping them improve in a specific aspect or in multiple aspects of their game. Remember, that will help them trust their own abilities. I believe that sometimes simply adjusting the player's perspective to make them feel better about themselves can be a powerful tool. Confidence begets confidence. If a player walks to the free-throw line confident that they will make the shot, it raises the odds that they will be successful. But I can't directly help them improve their self-confidence. (That's why it's called *self*-confidence.) Self-confidence comes from the person's trust and belief in their abilities to handle new or unfamiliar situations. However, I can influence their self-confidence indirectly. By creating a comprehensive development plan, by reinforcing their vision, and by helping them master specific skills, it stands to reason that they are positioned to develop greater self-confidence on their own.

FINDING THE GOOD IN PEOPLE

Self-esteem is a whole different ball game, and it gets into the psychology and emotions surrounding a person's opinion of their worth. Again, I believe that I can have an indirect influence on helping someone increase their self-esteem, and for me that is just as important as contributing to their self-confidence. When working with players, there are a few things that I try to do:

- Reinforce the unique attributes they have as a person (outside of basketball). Are they friendly? Are they respectful? Are they an intellectual? Do they have a good sense of humor? Are they accepting of others? Are they good with kids? Everyone has something good in them. I try to tell people what I see in them that is good.

- Believe in them. I assume that everyone I work with has the capacity to get better.

- Criticize carefully and professionally. Constructive feedback is critical, but the *how* and the *when* matter a great deal, and a little goes a long way. I believe in the three-to-one rule. Find three positives before you address the constructive criticism point.

- When they talk, listen. Let them know that you hear and understand them (which is not the same as agreeing with them).

- Adjust perspective. Show them that they are doing better than they thought.

I believe that these things build on one another: confidence, self-confidence, self-esteem. I also believe that it is a lifelong pursuit. When I lost my job at the University of Florida, my self-esteem took a hit. As I mentioned in chapter 1, I spent the rest of the year traveling around, trying to learn as much as I could about coaching by visiting sixteen different schools, watching their practices, talking to coaches, and attending their games. Toward the end of the journey, I spent four days in Tucson visiting legendary coach Lute Olson's practices. (Afterward, I understood why his University of Arizona teams had so much success over the years.)

Leaving Tucson, I headed back to LA, where I was staying with a good friend, Hal Erskine. By that time, I had spent three weeks in a rental car by myself, and I was getting too deep into my thoughts. On the highway that led directly through the Sonoran Desert, I began having a profound conversation with someone in the passenger seat who was, of course, not really there. I told this imaginary person to "think of the days you let slip by, / a beautiful sunset or a clear blue sky." These words flowed out of me as a poem. The theme was all about how precious life is and to take advantage of every moment you have. By the time I got to Yuma, I had completed a poem that I called "Carpe Diem." I pulled over at a truck stop and wrote it down so that I wouldn't forget it. (You can find that poem at the beginning of section 4 of this book.)

I had copies of the poem nicely printed up and gave them to friends (along with copies of Og Mandino's book *The World's Greatest Salesman*[25]). Why? Because I believe that all things in life boil down to levels. Levels of confidence, levels of understanding, levels of commitment, levels of integrity, levels of intensity, and levels of relationships. Social media has led us to believe that the more people you know and collect in your circle, the better. But it's not how many people you know that really matters; it's how you know them and how they know you to be. I thought that both my poem and Og's book sent that same message.

THE POWER OF THOUGHTFULNESS

The following year, I ended up coaching at Chaminade University in Honolulu, and I was living in an apartment the size of a closet on Waikiki Beach. One day there was a knock on the door, and it was a UPS delivery guy with a box for me from the National Society of Poetry. In the box was a letter telling me that my poem "Carpe Diem" was a top entry of the year, and it was accepted for publication in the book that was in the box. There was also a plaque with my poem on it and a minuscule check. At the end of the letter, it stated, "You can now consider yourself a published poet." It turns out that my mom and my sister Sharon submitted the poem without telling me.

Did that increase my confidence? Somewhat, because it was a sign that I was developing a skill. (Although I had no illusions that

---

25   Mandino, *The World's Greatest Salesman*.

I could quit coaching to become America's next poet laureate.) Did it increase my self-confidence? Yes, because poetry was entirely new to me, and it built up my sense of being able to do something totally unfamiliar. Did it increase my self-esteem? A little, because I felt like it expanded my value or worth in the world by a fraction.

This story is a reminder to me. For any of us who are involved in the business of helping people develop, our actions can have both a direct and an indirect impact on another person's perception of their own abilities. I'm sure that my mom and my sister didn't set out on a mission to build my confidence, self-confidence, or self-esteem by submitting that poem. But, indirectly, it did all three.

CHAPTER 15

MAINTAIN A QUALITY GROWTH ENVIRONMENT WITH ACCOUNTABILITY

If you put good people in bad systems you get bad results.

—Stephen Covey

An effective development plan can flourish in the right environment. By the same token, if critical elements are missing from the environment, specifically a growth mindset and a sense of accountability, even the best plan can fall short. In this chapter, I touch on some of the critical factors for creating the right environment.

PHYSICAL ENVIRONMENT

It seems basic, but I am a stickler for a clean floor. If I expect players to take the workout seriously and to push hard, they have to be able to start, stop, and make cuts. There is no more sickening feeling for a player than when they try to make a cut and they slip. It takes away the ability to have a high level of intensity in the workout. When I was working with players in LA, I always made sure that the old Men's Gym floor was clean. I would grab the big push mop and clean the court between workouts. It was also a way for me to connect with John Wooden. I have read that back in the day it was a common sight to see Coach Wooden doing the same thing years earlier on the very same court between his team's workouts.

This doesn't mean that the setting needs to be plush and luxurious. In fact, sometimes the opposite is better. Even though it is Hollywood fiction, I can't help but relate this to the movie *Rocky III*. By this time, Rocky Balboa has defended his heavyweight title several times and has become a famous celebrity. He goes into preparation for his last match before retirement, and instead of training in a gritty gym, he works out in a glitzy Las Vegas–style environment. He loses the fight to the challenger, Clubber Lang.

Rocky and Lang schedule a rematch, and this time around Rocky is more focused and accountable for his conditioning. He changes his mindset from an entitled superstar boxer to a guy who is thirsty again. Instead of working out in Las Vegas, he trains with Apollo Creed in Creed's spartan gym in LA. In the rematch in Madison Square Gardens, a hyperfocused Rocky knocks Lang out to regain the championship. Did I mention that this was Hollywood?

ELIMINATE DISTRACTIONS

Given the busy lives of NBA players, combined with the rising attention being paid to load management, you have to make the most of the time that you have with players. It helps to be able to conduct the workouts in an environment with minimal distractions. There will always be players messing around in the locker room, and there are people wandering around whatever facility you are using. I am accountable for using the players' time efficiently, so my approach has always been that once you step across the sideline and onto the practice court, there needs to be a mindset change. In maintaining a quality environment, the basketball classroom (the court) is sacred. You are here to get better. I am here to help you. Let's respect each other and get to work. That doesn't mean that you can't enjoy yourself. Most of these guys are in their twenties, so there is going to be some humor involved, and you can't overreact.

Before I joined the Suns and I was working with players in Los Angeles, I was conducting a session for a group of NBA centers, including Chris Dudley, who was a friend of mine and playing for the Knicks at the time. I was running them through a drill where I guarded them on the low blocks. Because these guys were huge, I used the equalizer during this drill. As I mentioned in a previous chapter, this consisted of a hockey stick with tape and padding all over the handle. I would use the equalizer to push and shove the players around under the basket to simulate game conditions. When they shot, I would use the hockey stick to try to block their shots. I heard someone behind me say, "Mind if I jump in the workout, Coach?" Standing there was seven-foot-one, 325-pound Shaquille O'Neal (years before I actually coached him).

I had never met him before but said, "Sure, Shaq. Come on in." Shaq let me push him around once or twice, then on the next play he put his shoulder down and into me, and I left the ground. I flew into the padded wall behind the goal, legs dangling in the air, the equalizer in hand, like a cartoon character. Shaq was laughing, as was everybody else who was watching, including me. Then I jumped up, and we got right back into the drill. Enjoy the laugh, but get back to the drill. From then on, I changed my defensive angle so that Shaq couldn't send me airborne again.

CONSISTENCY OF TEACHING PRACTICES

Development of any kind requires opportunities for the player to get in enough repetitions for the skill to become muscle memory and to develop the myelin in the brain. It also requires conducting the drills in a way that simulates the situation that the players will experience in a game. For example, if a player is trying to increase their free-throw shooting percentage, you wouldn't have them walk out onto the court and shoot one hundred free throws. Nobody does that in a game. You would have the player practice their free throws when they are tired from other drills, and you would have them shoot them in smaller batches.

VETERANS SET THE TONE

If you look back at NBA championship teams, you will typically see that their best player was also the hardest worker. The veteran stars set the tone for the quality and intensity of the workouts. They set the example, and they're pulling the other players to a higher focus and work ethic. All of a sudden, that becomes the workout standard for the team. It's one thing for a coach to get on a player for not hustling and quite another for the team's best player to call the guy out instead. When that happens, the guy slacking off thinks, *Well, he's doing it by example, and if he's the best player, I'd better buckle down if I want to play with him.* Kevin Garnett and Kobe were both legendary for embodying this work ethic and intensity. So was Steve Nash, Russell Westbrook, Tim Duncan, and Michael Jordan. I always knew that when I had Jalen Rose in a workout, his ability to raise the intensity and focus level would help me to provide a high-quality and intensive experience for the players because of his leadership.

There is an unattributed quote that rings true for me: "What you permit, you promote. What you allow, you encourage. What you condone, you own." If you're tolerating lack of focus, you're actually promoting it. You're accountable, but it's always enhanced by the people you have in the workout or the person doing the work. In the right situation, your best players are doing a lot of the coaching on the court as well.

> In the right situation, your best players are doing a lot of coaching on the court as well.

ESTABLISH A PREDICTABLE ROUTINE

Because the life of an NBA player requires so much travel, it is important that workouts provide a consistent time and place for the player to focus on improving any aspects of their game. For the sake of example, a road week when I coached for the Knicks might involve a player schedule that looks like the following (the coach and staff schedule would be much more involved due to the countless hours of meetings that were a part of any road trip):

Tuesday	Morning	Practice in New York
	Afternoon	Flight to Houston
	Evening	Arrive in Houston; bus to hotel
Wednesday	Morning	Practice/walk-through
	Afternoon	4:00: Early bus to venue (usually rookies and younger players) 5:00: Late bus to venue (usually veterans)
	Evening	Game versus Houston Flight to LA Arrive in LA; bus to hotel
Thursday	Morning	Practice/walk-through/film
	Afternoon	4:00: Early bus to venue 5:00: Late bus to venue
	Evening	Game versus LA Flight to Portland Arrive in Portland; bus to hotel
Friday	Morning	Practice/walk-through/film
	Afternoon	Day off
Saturday	Morning	Practice/walk-through/film
	Afternoon	4:00: Early bus to venue 5:00: Late bus to venue
	Evening	Game versus Portland Flight back to New York

Because there are so many moving parts, you want to set up a schedule that is predictable for the players so that they can continue to get their workouts in. At the same time, within that predictable routine, you have to vary the workout to prevent monotony and to introduce new challenges. One way to do this is to mix the approach. For example, you might have some of the workout provide focused one-on-one work. Then you would have them break into subgroups, with point guards in one group, shooting guards and forwards in another group, and bigs in their own group. Finally, you might work in full-team drills and scenarios to employ against the upcoming opponent. The idea is to continue to work on the skills and create a predictable routine but also to make it interesting by changing up how you do it.

SECTION 4:
THE PROCESS

CARPE DIEM

Think of the days you've let slip by,
A beautiful sunset or a clear blue sky.
For time is a treasure for all to share
we should treat every second as if it were rare.
Cherish each moment with all of your heart
Be excited in knowing it's a brand new start.
Every day's an opportunity for us to grow
being a warm, special person is all we should know.
For those wasting time with anger and hate
the future will bestow an unbelievable fate.
Choose to see the good in all that's before you
the choice is yours it's what you must do.
Why have others passed on and you still remain?
The answer is easy, your life's not in vain.
So look straight ahead at what you'll achieve
For the secret of each moment's that you believe.
Believe in the Lord and he'll set you free
and the wonders of life will be yours to see.

—Phil Weber

CHAPTER 16

EXECUTE THE PLAN

For every philosophical idea about how we're going to do things, there has to be a plan to get there, and we have to be able to execute it, first in practice and then in games.

—Nick Nurse

Once you've evaluated the player and created the plan, now the work begins. You've established a strong relationship and you've instilled a growth mindset. The vision of where you want to go is fully in place, you have discussed the standards, and you've established a quality learning environment. Now begins the time when you must reinforce that practice doesn't always make perfect.

I learned a saying in the eighth grade from the legendary high school coach Reverend Ed Visscher: "Practice doesn't make perfect; perfect practice makes perfect." I have repeated this thousands of times in my life. You can practice things perfectly wrong with a player, and if they are still talented and fortunate enough to make it all the way to the NBA, it's much harder to make corrections to their form than it would have been to just learn the right way in the first place.

EXECUTE AND EXPAND

The process is all about expanding, which includes expanding the knowledge base of both the player and the coach. To constantly grow, we need to always push for higher standards. We need to continuously look for ways to do all things better. You need to grow in the level of belief in the player, and the player must consistently increase the amount of confidence in themselves. The coach must always look for ways to keep the workouts fresh and challenging, with the highest level of focus and intensity.

This is where a coach can make the biggest difference by knowing and following the sequential steps to build that skill. You know how to break that skill down to its most elementary parts in order to build it back up. This is where you've created drills to teach that small part of the whole skill. This is where you are reinforcing the vision. This is where you are watching every move. This is where you are catching them doing it correctly. This is where you are looking for ways to build their confidence. This is where you make certain that they are 100 percent focused for every rep. This is where you are holding them to the highest standard of intensity and performance. And when doing this drill, to borrow one of Coach Spoelstra's favorite phrases, "You do it to nauseam."

Successfully executing the plan will be contingent on the player fully understanding what will ultimately get them to mastery. To reach the highest level, the player must fall in love with the process of improvement. The player must be open to learning, be completely focused, and embrace the fact that time, boredom, frustration, and pain are all part of this process. When a player's intense desire is to thrive in these types of situations, that's when they improve the quickest.

> To reach the highest level, the player must fall in love with the process of improvement.

PUSHING THROUGH THE GROWTH

There are no easy ways to attain high-level skills. It is true that some players are more athletically gifted, and it is also true that some players learn faster than others. Some people do have natural ability. But if someone believes that they can learn a skill and they are determined and focused, it may take a great deal of time, but I will bet my money on their improvement. The ability to observe, understand, and navigate through the challenges a player faces in their development separates good coaches from average coaches. I believe in the saying that when the will of the teacher goes up against the will of the student, the stronger will *always* prevails.

When you are working with players, the speed of improvement can vary significantly as you go through the process. Real improvement will take time. Sometimes it will come very easily, and other times it will be a serious struggle filled with roadblocks and frustration. When the great players hit those plateaus, they turn on even more intensity and focus. As a coach, this is when you need to observe and frame this struggle in such a way as to motivate and inspire them over this hurdle. This is critical because, as a coach, you know that there will be more hurdles ahead. Being able to overcome those hurdles is when the real breakthroughs happen.

Boredom and monotony are often a hurdle to jump when developing any skill. Players must understand that they need to rewire their brains so that they never have to think about that portion of the skill. When they have created so much additional myelin in their brains, then that skill will be automatic. If a player believes that they can go through the motions and expect quick development, all while their mind is wandering, they are way off base. Depending on the player you are developing, overloading their body or mind will invariably bring pain. In most situations, that pain comes with growth. When you lift weights, there is great tension, yet you grow. If you fight through it and get to the other side of the pain, it will always bring quality results and, perhaps more importantly, reinforce the awareness that pain is part of the development process.

Piece by piece, the player develops by working on specific elements of the skill but also by participating in some drills that focus on the complete motion of the skill. This part-then-whole method will allow you to break down the finer points of the skill while also allowing the player to see and feel what the skill should look like.

My dad was a coach at Cold Spring Harbor High School on Long Island, nine miles from our house in Northport. When I think back, I'm pretty sure that my drive to become a good player came from wanting to make my dad proud. I was that little kid, dressed in a miniature suit and tie at the end of my dad's team's bench, working as a ball boy. I started to dribble a basketball when I was four years old. I remember going into the basement in the winter and just dribbling for hours. The pole right smack in the middle of the basement became the defender as I got older, and eventually that pole had no chance against my spin move.

Ball handling is a great example to consider when we talk about executing our plan because it's easy to see how you start off with the basic dribble, then grow as you develop more deceptive dribbles, and ultimately expand into high-level combinations of dribbling. It's important to master the control of a simple dribble before you advance to the more complicated ones.

DEVELOPING THROUGH LAYERS

As we learn and develop a skill like dribbling, we have to hardwire it into the frontal cortex of our brain. When giving talks to basketball camps, I often ask for a volunteer to come up to the front of the group. I then ask them to untie both of their shoes. I say, "On your mark, get set, tie your left shoe in a different way." Invariably, the pace is quite slow as the camper navigates their lace and ultimately ties it. I then say, "On your mark, get set, tie your right shoe." The result, of course, is much quicker than when they tied their left shoe. Author Tony Robbins uses a quote that I love when he says that repetition is the mother of skill. It is so true, but, again, you have to do the repetition correctly.

All skills have what I call *layers of understanding*. When you are teaching a skill, I believe that it is extremely helpful to use as many of your senses as possible. For instance, when learning a combination dribble sequence, have the player listen to the rhythm of the bounces, feel the finger pads maneuver the ball, and look straight ahead or at the coach's hands as the coach changes the number of fingers they hold up.

As you advance in your skill level, you also realize that there are multiple ways to do the same skill, which gives you enhanced layers. For instance, in my ball-handling lecture, I explain that quickness is arguably a player's most important physical attribute. I ask the campers which of the following techniques they think is quickest. First, standing stationary, I bounce the ball from my waist. Then I establish a dribbling crouch and bounce it from my knees. When I ask which is faster, they always say from the knees. I then bounce the ball soft from waist high, and then, from the same height, I bounce it extremely hard, and once again I ask which is quicker. The harder dribble gets the vote. The point I am making with the campers is that a lower, harder dribble is quicker. And now, armed with that simple bit of information, they can practice it and become a much better ball handler and a faster player.

One of the big attractions at Golden State games is for fans to arrive early to witness Stephen Curry's pregame ball-handling routine. I can just imagine how many hours he has done that exact routine and how long it took him to get it locked in. As a player continually hardwires skills into their brain, they begin to broaden possible responses to different actions. It is in the process of executing a plan that you are always looking to gradually advance the level of skill in your workouts. Don't skip steps, but always look to take a step forward. Executing your plan should be a nonstop process of reinforcing a skill and then looking to expand.

We never stay the same. We are all either regressing or getting better.

CHAPTER 17

EVOLVE AND BE CREATIVE WITH THE PLAN

Everybody has a plan until they get
punched in the mouth.

—Mike Tyson

Any plan that you create for the development of another person must
be a living, breathing thing. You don't just create a plan and then
stick blindly to it over the rest of the season. The plan has to be
flexible enough to evolve and adapt as the player's skills grow and
develop. There are many elements that can create the need to evolve
the player's development plan.

LET'S GO TO THE VIDEO

One of the best tools for developing players is showing them how they are doing a particular skill, then providing them with examples of other players who do that thing well. There are many ways to use video, which could probably be a whole book in itself. One of the most productive uses, in my experience, is to have a player take you through their decisions step by step and watch it with them. In the review process, they often work through right and wrong decisions until the light goes on, and it often requires very little verbal feedback from the coach. A golden nugget of life is that the first step toward change is awareness, so any way you can make players aware of their decisions is critical to gaining a higher level of court awareness.

In a way, it's like the movie *Groundhog Day*. TV weatherman Phil Connors, played by Bill Murray, wakes up every day in some bizarre time loop in which the same thing happens over and over. Once he realizes what's going on, he decides to change the outcome for his own benefit. The main point here is that when Connors is able to see the problems he will encounter, he knows what is coming, and now that he has heightened awareness, he can change the outcome for his benefit.

Video is also helpful to show the fundamentals executed properly. This is greatly enhanced by using slow motion and other aspects of video technology as teaching tools. As I have stated many times in this book, all players are unique, and they don't all learn the same way. Having a way for players to see themselves doing something the right way or the wrong way with their own eyes has a big impact.

There is a well-known story among Duke basketball fans about the power of video to influence a player.[26] Coach Mike Krzyzewski

---

26   Seth Davis, *Getting to Us: How Great Coaches Make Great Teams* (New York: Penguin Books, 2018).

saw that his star point guard, Bobby Hurley, was getting a reputation in the league as a whiner. During his junior year, Coach K suggested to Hurley that he should be less reactive to referees' calls and just play ball. Hurley either didn't agree with his coach that he was a whiner, or if he did, he didn't think it was a big deal. Coach K had a video assistant go back through the season's game video and construct a highlight reel. Then he sat down with Hurley, and they watched a full five-minute montage of nothing but clips of Hurley pouting, whining, complaining, arguing, rolling his eyes, and dropping his head. That must have been a very long five minutes for Hurley, and Coach K didn't have to say a word. Hurley could not deny the effect that his attitude was having on the fans and on his teammates. In this case, pictures are definitely worth a thousand words. Hurley was able to work on controlling his reactions and went on to be one of the best college point guards ever.

MONITOR PROGRESS

All players are different, and they're going to learn at different speeds. As a result, the coach always has to push the envelope at the right speed. As I mentioned in chapter 11, the player development process is a lot like mountain climbing. You wouldn't want a player with low confidence and experience to overreach. You must provide adequate challenge for each player, but it is critical to recognize that each player will be climbing the mountain at a different pace.

How much do I want to push? Do I need to adapt the plan to be more aggressive with their development? Am I pushing them too hard and frustrating their progress? Are they not grasping the firm foundational things that need to come first? As Stephen Covey says, some things come before other things. Have we established the foundation this player needs to move ahead on the plan as originally created, or do we need to change it based on where they are right now? Once a coach starts working in a focused way with a player, they always learn more about the player in the process. Should I now be using different players for them to watch as examples? Again, this is where video is critical.

LEARN AGILITY

Not every player learns at the same rate. If a player is overwhelmed by the development plan, or if their progress is slower than you anticipated, you have to spend more time showing them what you need them to do. You don't make it a big deal. You just take a step back and really lock in and emphasize this one skill so that they can ultimately build on it. Often coaches make a mistake and realize that they have pushed players too far too quickly. They put them in calculus before they had algebra covered.

The opposite is true as well. Sometimes you create a plan that you quickly see is not keeping up with a player's ability to learn. When Amar'e Stoudemire came into the NBA in 2002, high school kids didn't have to play a year in college. The Suns drafted him in the first round directly from high school. He was athletic and talented but raw. I was shocked at how fast he learned. He developed so many big-time skills so quickly, including a jump hook that looked like he had been shooting it all his life. For a fast learner like Amar'e, you have to accelerate the plan to accommodate his learning style and to continue to challenge him.

OUTSIDE VARIABLES

Player development does not happen in a vacuum. The player is part of a larger system. In this case, they are members of a team and a larger organization. All teams have different variables, and the player should be developing on a trajectory that best helps the team. Things change. Players get injured, so lineups have to adjust, and the domino effect impacts everyone. Maybe now the player you are working with has to take on a completely different role. I believe in holistic development with points of emphasis. You want to be a star in your role? How does that happen? There are certain things that you're going to be asked to do. All of a sudden, your role is different and you're going to be asked to do different things. It may be short term or long term. The development plan has to evolve to meet the changing needs of the team.

> Player development does not happen in a vacuum. The player is part of a larger system.

Shawn Marion was the ninth pick in the first round of the draft pick for the Suns. He joined the league as a small forward and was immediately a walking double-double. I believe that nine out of ten coaches would have played Shawn at the small forward position for his entire career. We found that he was more effective in what we called the *skilled forward* position. It was unconventional to play someone with Shawn's physical makeup at what most traditionally called the *power forward*. That was a major change in skills and focus. The plan must consider the necessary skill sets and evolve to accommodate the needs of the team for that particular player. The players and coaches must be flexible to keep the plan current. Shawn thrived in the role and went on to become a four-time NBA All-Star.

THINK CREATIVELY

Because all players are different and their roles on their teams are different, sometimes creativity is required as part of a player's development. One of my favorite stories about this subject is from Steve Kerr when he was the Suns GM. One day during the 2007–2008 season, Steve and I were discussing player development after a practice. Steve told me that when he played for the Portland Trailblazers, he worked out occasionally with a player development coach named Chip Engelland. (As an assistant coach for San Antonio, Engelland is well known for his ability to help players improve and is probably best known for working in San Antonio with Tony Parker's and Kawhi Leonard's shots.) Steve described his role in Portland as a sporadic bench player. What Steve didn't say but that readers should know is that he played on five NBA championship teams and is the best three-point shooter in NBA history.

In a creative approach to replicating Steve's role on the team, Engelland would sit with Steve on the bench during an individual workout. Then, every few minutes, he would have Steve jump up and run down the floor. Engelland would pass the ball to him, and Steve would take a three-point shot. Engelland said that because it was in the middle of the season, conditioning was not an issue. They would replicate game conditions for Steve by taking only three-point shots, one shot at a time. Steve said that he might take nine shots in practice coming in off the bench instead of the usual hundreds of shots, one after the other, using only a rebounder to throw the ball to him. They kept track of Steve's shooting percentage, and the number steadily increased. He said that approach prepared him physically with his shot and mentally for his role with the Trailblazers.

There are several things to learn from that story. First, each player is different, and the plan has to fit the player. Second, Coach

Engelland took the time to really understand Steve and his unique role within the team structure. Third, it worked because Steve trusted Coach Engelland and he had 100 percent buy-in to the plan. Lastly, sometimes you have to get creative to make a plan useful to both the player and the team.

CHAPTER 18

INVOLVE THE OVERLOAD PRINCIPLE

We are what we repeatedly do.

—Aristotle

When working with a player to develop specific skills, many coaches rely on something called the *overload principle*. An overload drill is designed to put a higher-than-normal mental or physical stress level on a player to enhance their learning and speed up their development process. Focused overload drills are designed to concentrate on specific muscle groups to develop them more intentionally and quickly. Most sports fans have seen this principle in use when a baseball player is waiting on deck to take their turn at the plate. They take warm-up swings with a weighted metal ring called a *donut* slipped onto the barrel of the bat. If you ever want to see a bunch of crazy gadgets, go to a sports trade show someday. There are more bizarre contraptions being marketed to help players of all sports than you can imagine.

Would I ever introduce some kind of sports-related apparatus into one of my player workouts? Guilty as charged! At the same time that I moved to LA and began working with NBA players, I read a long article in *Sports Illustrated* about Michael Jordan's workouts. Michael was using a series of weighted basketballs provided by his trainer for rebounding drills. The idea was that it would build his hand and forearm strength.

HEAVY DUTY

I ordered one of the six-pound balls immediately after reading the article. (A normal basketball weighs just less than one and a half pounds.) I started using this weighted ball immediately in the same way that Michael was using it—to snatch the heavy ball off the backboard, pivot, and make an outlet pass. But my mind didn't stop there. I was working with Tyus Edney, who was a great player in college for UCLA and who was most famous for his full-court dribble and buzzer-beating layup against Missouri in the NCAA tournament. The Bruins went on to win the title that year. When I worked out with him, he was with the Sacramento Kings. Tyus was a quick point guard and a good scorer. The one thing that drove me crazy about his shot was the way he would bring it up off the dribble. He simply bent too far over to bring up the ball, almost down at court level. What was the problem with that? It made his shot include a windup, so it was slow compared to a normal, more efficient motion. I had him start practicing his shot using the six-pound ball. My thinking was that he should shoot it against the backboard a couple of thousand times, and the weighted ball would lock in a more efficient motion and do it faster than using a normal basketball. It worked. Tyus eliminated the excess motion in his shot, which became quicker due to the reduced motion.

When I worked with Tyus, he would end all his sessions shooting his heavy ball against the backboard. That reminded me of a device I saw demonstrated by legendary Celtic Jo Jo White between games of a Final Four weekend. The way the device worked was that you placed your elbow underneath a ball that was hinged to provide resistance. The motion of your arm was secured so that you would always follow through up and straight using perfect form. I really liked the concept but felt that it was unrealistic to have players spend the necessary amount of time it would take to use this device. Then it dawned on me to simply shoot the six-pound ball into the basket instead of against the backboard in order to see the proper trajectory as the ball went through the hoop.

The first time I used the heavy ball to help a player with their shot was when I worked with Jalen Rose when he was with the Indiana Pacers. Jalen was six foot eight, long armed, and truly multidimensional. His game would fit seamlessly into today's play. During all those summer workouts in the old Men's Gym at UCLA, Jalen was always one of the hardest workers. He brought maturity and leadership to whatever workout he was involved in. If I was driving the players for more intensity, Jalen would always have my back, and I loved the spark that he brought to the work I was doing with players. When Jalen was in the group, we would end every session with a one-on-one workout in which he shot the heavy ball. Our goal was to reduce his motion a bit and to adjust his wrist placement.

That summer, Jalen and I worked out for seven weeks. There were many factors in Jalen's tremendous improvement the following season, and his hard work was easily at the top of the list. He was also being used differently by new coach Larry Bird. Larry saw where Jalen could help the team the most. He also had a roster filled with some great players. I would like to think that his improved stroke, aided by working out with the heavy ball, had something to do with Jalen earning the NBA's Most Improved Player Award for the 1999–2000 season. That same season, I watched him courtside from the coach's seat in my NBA break-in year with the Phoenix Suns.

OVERLOAD IMPACT

Let's examine why the overload drills (in this case, weighted balls) worked. First, we did this drill at the very end of the workout when the player was already fatigued. Second, it was using the same musculature as with a regular basketball. I do not have any scientific proof that this builds myelin faster, which in turn develops the skill better, but I do know that Joe Johnson shot an impressive 48 percent from three-point range in 2004–2005 after working out by shooting the nine-pound ball twelve feet from the basket. Whenever he missed one, it sounded like the rim was going to break.

Ball handling is another area where I used these weighted balls as an overload drill. When I arrived in Phoenix, I used some of the Suns' training budget to buy twelve Ooofballs. We picked up four four-pound balls, four six-pound balls, and four nine-pound balls. The four-pound balls would bounce, but they were extremely heavy relative to the normal leather basketball. For Shawn Marion, who could do so many amazing things on the basketball court, ball handling was one of our main focus points for his first three years.

Every player I worked with had a goal to create a hard, tight handle, meaning they would have extremely strong forearms. The ability to have a low, hard dribble when they needed one was a tremendous advantage offensively.

Shawn and I spent many quality minutes during each workout performing all aspects of ball handling, but the drill that required him to dribble two four-pound balls at the same time would make anyone's forearms cry. Executing the drill with proper body mechanics and pushing the dribble down as hard as you can really create a high level of intensity and muscle fatigue. Shawn was a hard worker, and he stayed at it. As a result, he continually improved.

There are also many examples of the overload principle outside of basketball. In his book *The Talent Code*, Daniel Coyle discusses how the modified soccer game, futsal, has helped create many Brazilian soccer stars.[27] Why? Because the sport is played with a smaller ball on an undersize, hard court. This makes for a much faster game and requires players to develop lightning-quick reflexes and superior ball-handling skills. The overload principle is a great technique to have in your tool kit to help players concentrate on and accelerate their development in specific, focused ways.

---

27 Coyle, *The Talent Code*.

CHAPTER 19

MAINTAIN EFFICIENCY AND INTENSITY LEVELS

Hard work beats talent when talent fails to work hard.

—Kevin Durant

Everything in the game of basketball is interrelated. Offense depends on and influences defense, and vice versa. Former Indiana coach Bobby Knight used to claim that coaches talk about only two things: offense and defense. And they neglect the third, more important, thing: the transition from offense to defense and defense to offense. Working on general skill development and improving on all aspects of the game are vital, regardless of position. But, in my opinion, what cannot be overlooked with teams is understanding how to integrate and focus on certain skills to maximize offensive and defensive efficiency. The same kind of evaluation should be done as an overall team assessment.

THE INTENSITY LEVEL SHOULD FIT THE PLAYER

In chapter 10, we discussed player evaluation and its importance in creating an effective plan. Coaches must first use a lens that allows them to reach a deep understanding of where the skill sets of each of the team's players are at the moment. Second, they need to make a determination of the physical and mental attributes of each player. Third, they need to decide which of those traits can be improved most easily and which have a lower ceiling. That might feel like a tedious activity, to break it down into such detail, but only by doing so can you help the athlete get to where they can become the best player possible. To reach this degree of maximum efficiency, there are many layers of information regarding that particular team that must be taken into account as well.

The next step is to develop an offense and defense that you can build that matches the players' abilities within your own philosophy. This requires an understanding of the many offensive and defensive possibilities available that can lead to maximum efficiency. Through repetition, you work on improving all skills holistically. In addition, you focus on the ones that specifically match the physical attributes, the skill sets, and the mental makeup of your team. You then work to reinforce (with confidence and positive feedback) that you will reach higher and higher levels of efficiency each and every day. It's all about constant improvement and establishing a growth mindset.

You might read this and say, "Well, sure, that's all just common-sense coaching." Not so fast. Let's take, for example, Amar'e Stoudemire. We had plenty of basketball-savvy people telling us to post him down low due to his size and limited shooting range. Because we chose not to follow convention, we received a lot of criticism at first. Early in Amar'e's career, he was very strong in his upper body and could jump out of the gym, but he had very little body mass from his waist down. Later, Robin Pound, the strength coach for the Suns, said that Amare'e has "designer genes." But early in his NBA career, whenever he did a post-up down low, it was easy for defenders to push him off the blocks. All the focus in the world was not going to quickly change Amar'e's body or the way that teams started to defend him in the post once they discovered that they could push him away from the basket. On the other hand, we knew that Amar'e was extremely quick, so he could beat most defenders with one dribble. By simply moving him higher up in the paint to the elbow of the free-throw lane, opposing teams could not load up defensively. That made him more comfortable but not necessarily more efficient.

Then, as we had hoped, some things started to work in combination. We committed to that offensive change and then used a laser focus in his development. We worked intensively on his offensive skills on that part of the court. He started to get more comfortable and increased his scoring, averaging twenty-six points per game. In addition, this helped our offense become more efficient. We still worked hard on low-post moves, but the main focus was on his work higher in the paint.

USE FOCUS INTERVALS

This leads to a key principle. You could force a player to stay on the court and work out all day long, but any player has a limited amount of time that they can practice with maximum intensity. As I have noted many times already, all players are different. It is critical to thoroughly assess the players on your roster. Those who can move the efficiency needle the most are the highest priority. Then, with laser focus on specific skill development, incorporate them collectively with the correct offensive and defensive vision. It is also imperative that the complementary players are empowered in their roles and that their skill development matches perfectly with their corresponding roles.

Coaching is about creating an intense environment for improvement while maximizing those minutes so that the team as a whole can reach its highest level of efficiency. Talent level matters—no question. A coach has an advantage when the team's best players are the hardest workers, a trait common to NBA championship teams. Steve Alford, a teammate of Michael Jordan's on the 1984 US Olympic team, said that there was a huge gap between Michael Jordan's skill set and everyone else's on the team. Yet every day at practice, Michael was the first player on the court and the last player to leave. It's no coincidence that Michael and Kobe shared that habit.

> Coaching is about creating an intense environment for improvement while maximizing those minutes so that the team as a whole can reach its highest level of efficiency.

A strong team culture that integrates levels of focus on individual player development in concert with the team's offensive and defensive philosophies will maximize the team's efficiency. This is particularly true if coaches include constant and empowering reinforcement of all the positive results they see in both individual and team development.

CHAPTER 20

ANALYZE AND ADJUST STANDARDS

It takes three things to be a "special" player:
talent, character, and competitive fire.

—Kevin Eastman

A key part of the process should be monitoring, analyzing, and continually adjusting upward the standards that you have for the player you're working with. The work that power forward Loy Vaught and I did one summer when he was with the Clippers is a good example. We would change up the beginning of his daily workouts to keep them fresh, but we still ended each session with him making five shots in a row as we went through a standard set of shooting drills based on how the Clippers were using him offensively. He had to hit five in a row before he could move on to the next action. As the summer progressed, Loy made great strides. We increased the number of makes needed on that series of shots as his confidence grew. We incrementally adjusted upward all summer until Loy needed to make ten in a row when we reached September. The early portion of our workouts always branched out into other drills, each with different standards. We built increasing pressure into these drills because when you got to the money ball (the last shot he had to make to move on), the pressure increased naturally, with a miss sending him back to zero. As his ability to make consecutive shots grew over the summer, so did the amount of confidence Loy had in his shot. Making ten shots in a row consistently had an enormous effect on Loy's self-assurance.

INCREASE EXPECTATIONS UNIQUELY

Steadily increasing standards is the simplest and most tangible way to see growth. The standards that a player sets for themselves will dictate how far they can go. Increasing what is expected will always be embraced by the great ones. They crave that next plateau. I created a corny expression for the players to remember, urging them to become "con men." To me, it is a formula that builds on itself. If you use consecutives in your training, automatically you increase the level of concentration. Once you raise your level of concentration automatically, you will become more consistent. When you become more consistent, automatically you get an abundant supply of what all great shooters have: confidence. On one of our last workout days

> Steadily increasing standards is the simplest and most tangible way to see growth.

before Loy left for training camp with the Clippers, I let him keep going after he hit the required ten in a row, and he proceeded to make nineteen consecutive shots. After he finally missed, Loy turned to me and said with a smile, "Coach, once you get all that confidence, then you get a big contract!"

But … you guessed it—all players are different. The way that you set and adjust standards has to fit the player you are developing. What worked for Loy might be counterproductive for another player. For example, for a player who is not yet a proficient shooter, the consecutive-shot requirement might not work until they are further along in their development. That drill might instead frustrate and demotivate them, thereby chipping away at their confidence. You do want to challenge the player but with an appropriate task that makes sense for their skills and role.

Setting and adjusting standards becomes critical to help players understand how to use their skills in a way that fits the team. I learned a great example of this when I was the head coach for the Sioux Falls Skyforce, the G League team for the Miami Heat. One night, one of my players scored a team-record fifty-two points in a game. That was an impressive number, and the player was getting frustrated that he wasn't getting a call-up to the NBA. But when you looked more closely at his stats, his assist-to-turnover ratio wasn't good, and neither was his three-point percentage. I tried to help him understand that a call-up depends not only on his skills but also on the needs of the team. I explained that the Heat didn't need someone to get called up to play like Dwyane Wade. They needed someone who could come and play *with* Dwyane Wade.

SET THE EXAMPLE

It is critical to push the envelope forward in the spectrum of a player's basketball and personal development. Are you doing everything you can as a coach? Key to continuously improving the work you do with players is having a growth mindset of your own. Constantly ask yourself the following questions:

- In what ways can I tangibly increase what is expected today?

- What goals can we strive for today?

- In what new ways can I challenge the player today?

The other major part of this step is being open to the input of others. It is important to ask for the player's opinion of how they think the development plan is working. Do changes need to be made based on their perspective? It is also important to be open to the input of other coaches or staff members who know the player's skills and the team context.

I teach players a series of footwork moves that I learned from Kiki VanDeWeghe. Kiki was an All-Star and a prolific scorer during his NBA career, and he and I operated some summer basketball camps together. During the camp, he taught a very useful footwork series, and he was able to break it down in a way that the camp attendees (and I) could really understand. As a result, every single player I have worked with since then has benefited from Kiki's knowledge because I was open to learning from him. I always try to continue to grow to be a better coach and to find better ways to help players develop. So often those ideas are out there somewhere, being used by someone else. Ask for suggestions, opinions, and feedback about what you are currently doing and be open to new and different ideas.

CHAPTER 21

REINFORCE AND EXPAND THE VISION

Do not let what you cannot do interfere with what you can do.

—John Wooden

This section of the book has addressed how player development involves the mental as well as the physical. We must not only reinforce the vision the player has for where they want to go but also expand the vision.

UNDERSTANDING YOUR
ABILITY TO INFLUENCE

One of the hardest things we have to do as coaches is to help a player think in terms of their sphere of influence. Stephen Covey does a terrific job of explaining this concept in his book *The 7 Habits of Highly Effective People*.[28] I have quite possibly shown this to every NBA player I have ever coached because it's powerful in its simplicity. In basketball, there is so much that a player is not in control of. They aren't in control of the referees. They aren't in control of the Twitter trolls. They aren't in control of the fans. They aren't directly in control of their teammates. They aren't in control of the other team's game plan. This is what Covey calls the *circle of concern*—things that a player might worry about but can't control.

What can the player control?

- Conditioning

- Work ethic

- Effort

- Mindset

- Focus

- Attitude

- Energy

These are just a few examples of the things that fall into what Covey calls the *circle of influence*—the things the player can control. By definition, the universe of the circle of concern will always be bigger than the circle of influence. There are many more things in the world that you cannot control than things that you can. The idea is to not allow your

---

28   Covey, *The 7 Habits of Highly Effective People*.

mental energy and focus to drain away by fixating on the things that you can't control. Instead, lock in on the things that you can control.

circle of concern
circle of influence

This concept is simple but very powerful. Your circle of influence correlates directly to the amount of power you have in the world. Unfortunately, according to Covey, many people spend too much time and energy focusing on things they have no control over—those things in their circle of concern. When that happens, it tends to put people into a reactive position and a victim mindset, reducing their personal power. They spend all their energy worrying that other people are doing those things that limit them. Focusing on the things they don't control can send them into a mindset of blaming, criticizing, and behaving negatively toward other people, including teammates. John Wooden used to say, "Do not let what you cannot do interfere with what you can do."

circle of concern
circle of influence

By comparison, focusing on their circle of influence helps players be more proactive and take control of their condition. When they do that, their circle of influence grows larger—in other words, the amount of power they have in the world increases. It has been my practice to share Covey's circles with every player I work with because the picture shows how, if a player simply focuses on what they can control, it will give them the ability to improve more rapidly.

When I think back over my own life, I remember the period of time when I was out of coaching. I knew that I could help players develop, and I knew that the way I did it was effective (inside my circle of influence). I didn't consider my work with players in the old Men's Gym at UCLA to be a business, because with a business, you charge people for what you are doing. I did it because it was my passion and because I could see that others benefited from my work with them (inside my circle of influence). I did not worry that I wasn't with a team (outside my circle of influence). I didn't stress about the fact that, at the time, the idea of a player development business didn't exist yet (outside my circle of influence). I stayed focused on helping and learning from the best players in the game, so I was constantly improving my craft (inside my circle of influence).

By focusing on and working hard within my circle of influence, it got larger, and my circle of concern got smaller, which is the goal. Because we tend to spend more energy, time, and focus on whichever circle is larger, we want to maximize the size of the circle of influence and minimize the size of the circle of concern. Concentrating intensely on my circle of influence was a direct factor that led me to go from being out of coaching to having a seat on the bench in the NBA.

The idea is always to help the player understand where to focus their energy and attention, and Covey's circles have worked well for me in explaining this concept to players.

circle of concern
circle of influence

CORRECT AND MOTIVATE THROUGH THE PLAN

One question that I like to ask players every day during their workouts is, "Where do you think you are right now compared to where you expected to be by this time?" How players develop and the speed at which they do so vary across different areas of the game. A major component of the process will be your daily monitoring of where they think they are, how they feel about their progress, and what you can do to help them accelerate their development if needed. Remember that as you go through the workout with the player, you're consistently empowering them, catching them doing things correctly, and calling them out. For your part, you continue to adapt your approach to find the best way to get the player to understand whatever lesson or skill you're focusing on in that moment.

QUESTIONS FOR BOTH THE COACH AND THE PLAYER

The questions you ask yourself during the process are so important. Some of the questions that I return to while developing any player include the following:

- How can I help the player see that they are improving in this area?

- What is the best way for the player to be aware of their intensity level and to take it up a notch if necessary?

- Is there a teaching method I have not tried that will instill more confidence in the player?

- How can I break down that drill so that the player experiences greater success?

I have been privileged to work with many great players over the course of my coaching career. One thing that many of these exceptional athletes have in common is their intense inner drive. In their cases, sometimes a simple paradigm shift is all that's needed. With Joe Johnson, it was helping him visualize the perfect jump shot. With Amar'e Stoudemire, it was constantly explaining the importance of the jump shot from the elbow of the lane and how it would expand his entire arsenal. Subtle shifts in how players see themselves or a skill they need can allow them to expand and reach another plateau. It's the constant searching for that new way to reach a player that keeps coaching so inspiring to me.

> Subtle shifts in how players see themselves or a skill they need can allow them to expand and reach another plateau.

CHAPTER 22

MONITOR SELF-TALK

You only have control over three things in your life—the thoughts you think, the images you visualize, and the actions you take.

—Jack Canfield

This point in the player development process is the right place to ask yourself some questions that you might not have considered.

- Have you had an impact on your player's language?

- Do you constantly monitor what the player says and how they say it?

- Are you setting an example for the player to emulate?

- How does the player deal with frustration?

THE LANGUAGE OF PROGRESS

It is not unusual for players to get frustrated or to feel like they have hit a wall of some kind. Maybe they can't perfect a drill or achieve the number of successful reps you have set as a standard. As coaches say, they're stuck in the mud. This is a great time to take stock of your own approach, because it is how we are in the moments of adversity that define us. As British philosopher James Allen so eloquently states, "Circumstances do not make a man, they reveal us."[29] It is in these moments that you see what your player is made of.

If a player is struggling and you cave in and let them move to the next drill, you are allowing the player to let the adversity win, and a small piece of their self-worth is chipped away. By comparison, fighting through such situations by doing whatever it takes to accomplish the results that you both set for that drill will increase a player's belief in themselves and their ability to accomplish challenging tasks.

THE POWER OF THOUGHT

We are in control of 100 percent of our thoughts. The question is, Do we choose to understand and control our thoughts? We have the individual capacity to create empowering, inspiring thoughts. Period.

> We have the individual capacity to create empowering, inspiring thoughts.

As we hold those empowering thoughts, our minds become like a fertile garden. The things we think about continue to grow stronger and faster. This builds a positive momentum, and things start happening in your life that you never expected. It is a little bit

---

29   Allen, *As a Man Thinketh*.

like an old-fashioned flywheel. It takes considerable effort to get it turning and up to speed, but once there, the momentum makes it easy to keep it going.

This does not happen by itself. Just like the farmer who gets up early to tend to their crops, fertilizing, irrigating, and getting rid of the weeds, we need to monitor our every thought. Conversely, if we have negative and disempowering thoughts, they will strangle the positive ideas, goals, and dreams that we wish to grow. Do we focus on problems or solutions? Do we focus on things we can control? Or do we focus on what others think and do, giving away our personal power, as described in the previous chapter?

As a coach, I need to listen carefully to a player's language. What clues can I get about their mindset and progress from the words they use? How can I help them use language that is more affirming? We are constantly using affirmations, whether we use that word or another to identify our thoughts. Our thoughts constantly affirm who we are and what we believe. This process began upon our birth and will continue until we leave this earth. Where these affirmations come from and why people use them differently depends on many factors. Some of it connects back to self-esteem, as I addressed in chapter 14. Much of it is environmental. Our ideas, limitations, and beliefs about who we are have been shaped by friends, family, and random experiences; some have even been shaped by choice.

THE LESSONS OF HOME

When I think back over my own experience and reflect on some of the many, many interactions that shaped my inner voice, I recall two family interactions that are always in the back of my mind. They happened separately but built off each other to have a powerful impact on my inner voice. Both occurred in 1999 when I went home to Long Island to spend the week with my family.

As was customary in our family, someone would always volunteer to pick me up when my flight landed. I was happy to see that this time it was my dad and that he was willing and able to squeeze a run to the airport into his always busy workday. Once in the car, our conversation went straight to what I was doing with my life, as it always did. (Remember that by this time I had been in coaching, then out of coaching, then back in coaching. Now I was training NBA players in the summer and working with my buddy Brett Bearup, which included coaching a high school All-Star team on an awesome trip every summer.)

I was so excited to tell him about all the big-time players I had been working with at the old Men's Gym at UCLA. Instead of being impressed, Dad could not understand how I was working with all these wealthy players and agents and not getting paid. I told him that I was learning and making tremendous contacts. I also told him that I had developed two strong beliefs. First, if you work to reach a certain level of expertise, eventually the compensation will match your skill level. Second, if you help others get what they want without the expectation of receiving anything back from them, eventually you get what you want, and magic can happen.

He wasn't buying it. Looking back now, I can just imagine how that must have sounded to a guy who had worked so hard to build a business one step at a time. I know that what he said next came from his deep love for me. "Phil, I just don't want you to become a basketball bum." I had been playing basketball my entire life. I have spent most of my waking hours around the sport, and therefore I have been around "basketball people" of every description. This includes the people who seem to be captured in some vague but unproductive permanent orbit around the sport. I knew exactly what Dad was saying. That discussion, and seeing it through my dad's eyes, reinforced what I didn't want to happen to me. Most importantly, it pushed me to continue to focus on what I did want. It gave me the fuel to make sure he ultimately saw that I was not wasting my time.

A second interaction that substantially influenced me came at the end of that same trip. On the last day of my visits, it is customary for me to take my mom out to breakfast before I head off. We chose Otto's Diner in our beautiful village of Northport, nestled in a little harbor on the north shore of Long Island. It was a magnificent summer day, so after breakfast we decided to take a walk along the L-shaped pier. My memory of this is so clear that I could show you the spot where we were standing when I told my mom, "I don't know what's going to happen next, but for the last three weeks, I've had this extremely strong feeling that something amazing is about to happen for me."

It was shortly after I returned to LA that Danny Ainge and I sat in the old Men's Gym at UCLA and he hired me as an assistant coach. As I described in chapter 2, I went from completely out of coaching to a seat on an NBA bench. Sometime later, my mom surprised me by sending me a beautiful picture of that pier for my wall. That picture is a reminder to live with positive thoughts and high expectations.

I return to the metaphor about a garden. Who plants the weeds? Just like that garden, our minds absorb negative thoughts that limit us and that can strangle our goals and dreams. And just like that farmer who is tending their crops, we must pay attention to what we are doing. We must be disciplined and aware of where our thoughts are at all times and realize that what we think about grows. We should create an environment and mindset that we sow with seeds focused on growth, gratitude, solutions, service, and love. Decide, be disciplined, and take joy in seeing your harvest multiply beyond what you could ever have imagined.

CHAPTER 23

REDUCE LIMITING BELIEFS

Whether you think you can, or you think you can't—you're right.

—Henry Ford

To what extent does the belief that something is beyond human limits influence an athlete's mentality? There are many barriers that can impact a player's effectiveness. The one I try to work with the most is between the athlete's ears. A coach must watch for indications that a player is creating negative thoughts and actions that will reduce the effectiveness of the practice or workout. That became apparent to me even more when I read Denis Waitley's book *The Psychology of Winning.*[30] I always say that I try to be a Geiger counter to limiting beliefs, and when I detect them, I owe

---

30   Waitley, *The Psychology of Winning.*

it to the player (or to any person I'm with, for that matter) to address them.

THE IMPOSSIBLE BARRIER

One of my favorite stories in sports history, and one that I have held in my mind for most of my career, is that of Sir Roger Bannister breaking the four-minute-mile barrier. In the modern sports era, it was considered impossible for a human to run a mile in under four minutes. Even the most well-conditioned human body simply was not capable. People assumed that if it was possible, someone would have already done it. Some runners got close, but nobody could break four minutes. The record of 4:01.4 had stood for nine years.

On May 6, 1954, in Oxford, England, Roger Bannister broke the record. Bannister, a doctor in training, ran a 3:59.4 mile. Breaking that milestone was a monumental athletic accomplishment on many levels, but that's not why I tell the story. After breaking the record that had stood for nine years, Bannister's new record of 3:59.4 stood for exactly forty-six days. Today more than a thousand runners have surpassed the four-minute-mile record, including some high school students. Roger Bannister tipped over the first domino on what was considered an unachievable goal, and a mental barrier was lifted in the minds of all milers.

> The barriers we construct are frequently barriers only in our minds.

It was not a physical barrier that kept runners from beating the four-minute mark for so many years. There was not some sort of leap in physical ability that allowed so many runners to follow

Bannister. It was the change in mindset that made the difference. The barriers we construct are frequently barriers only in our minds. The same thing holds true with basketball players. If they think a goal is unattainable, then that is their reality. It is my responsibility as a coach to help them get rid of the limiting beliefs that hold them back from being the best player they can be.

I fully realize that I am no Nostradamus, but I have found that some of my early basketball prophecies have played out. Since roughly 2004, I have been bringing up a couple of points in relation to the NBA three-point line. To me, it has been the basketball equivalent to the four-minute mile. There are two things that I believed. First, the three-point line on a basketball court, until recent history, has represented a limiting belief. There was a time when the three was relatively new and coaches and front office staff doubted that players would ever be physically adept and skilled enough to score consistently from that distance for it to be a dependable game strategy. Second, I fully believed that any shots we practice intensely (including three-pointers from twenty-five feet) are good shots to take in a game. It's hard to believe that this was radical thinking in 2004. I've always thought that if you could go back in time to 2004 and show people a game played today that featured Stephen Curry, Trae Young, Klay Thompson, or James Harden, they would be stunned to see how far away players are shooting from now and the way that three-pointers can dominate game strategy nowadays.

How many limiting beliefs do you have in your own life? What limiting beliefs do you allow to perpetuate with your players? How can you eliminate both? These are powerful questions that you should take the time to fully examine. I have made the point several times in this book that people are the culmination of their thoughts, which takes me back to Roger Bannister. Former mile world record holder Sebastian Coe said, "Roger Bannister is the best example of someone doing something where your brain says 'no' but your heart says 'yes, you can.'"[31]

31   *Bannister: Everest on the Track*, directed by Tom Ratcliffe and Jeremy Mosher (Newtown, PA: Virgil Films, 2016), DVD.

CHAPTER 24

LEVERAGE MINDFULNESS

One thing I've learned as a coach is that you can't force your will on people. If you want them to act differently, you need to inspire them to change themselves.

—Phil Jackson

In the last chapter, we discussed the importance of ridding the mind of thoughts that limit your progress. The next step is to take a deeper dive into how mindfulness can influence our condition. Specifically, I am going to talk about the importance of meditation. Let me begin by saying three things right off the bat. First, some of you will immediately skip to the next chapter. How do I know that? Because I would have done the same in years past. I would have been skeptical about a chapter on meditation in a book allegedly written about personal and cultural development. Second, I am not an expert. My position on the subject is a result of my experience and research. Third, from my personal experience, it really works.

THE NEXT FRONTIER

Athletes have always looked for innovations that can give them an edge, and that has never been truer than today. In the past, the primary focus has been (and remains) on helping a player grow physically. The thinking was that if an athlete can get stronger and faster, they will play better. It's hard to argue with that. Then, over time, other lifestyle and health practices gained attention. For example, many athletes today are obsessive about sticking to their sleep routine. The other development opportunity is diet, probably made most famous recently by NFL quarterback Tom Brady and his unique food regimen. But the aspect that I want to focus on in this chapter is the mental side of player development. Surprisingly, sports teams have been paying attention to the mental aspect of player effectiveness for a long time. Chicago Cubs owner Philip Wrigley hired a psychologist to work with his players as far back as the 1930s. But this idea didn't gain much traction or become widely noticed until much more recently.

In fact, the interest in the mental aspect of sports spawned the modern profession called *sports psychology*. At first, players had to get over the stigma of "seeing a shrink" before they engaged with sports psychologists. Like a lot of things, all it took was a couple of world-class athletes to go public about how much working with one helped them win an NBA championship, World Series, Super Bowl, Masters, or Wimbledon. All of a sudden, high-profile sports psychologists had all the business they could handle. Nowadays there are even parents hiring sports psychologists to help their kids play better in youth sports.

THE MIND/BODY CONNECTION

What lies beyond the mental aspect of the game? What is the next frontier? In my opinion, diving deeper into understanding the mind is the next frontier. Meditation, the quieting of our mind, has been shown to have tremendous impact on the lives of those who consistently practice it. If you are new to meditation, that might sound a little out there to you. Stick with me.

Why is it important to be open to something like this? Albert Einstein suggested that we can't solve problems by using the same kind of thinking we used when we created them. He was a proponent of new ideas and new thinking. That is how I think about meditation. To me, it is like the analogy of the way a computer operates. At the bottom there is software, then a platform, then the infrastructure. With people, there are beliefs, then there are feelings, then there are behaviors. Meditation can help you get beneath all of it. There are a lot of people who advocate for meditation, but as I mentioned briefly in chapter 6, it was Joe Dispenza who demystified it for me. In his book *Breaking the Habit of Being Yourself,* Dispenza presents the science behind the effect that meditation can have on the performance and physical changes of the brain.[32] For me, it moved meditation into science and out of the mystical realm. He explains that the majority of our brain's function is to act as a depository of our past. It includes, out of necessity, the records of the things we have learned intellectually over the course of our lifetime.

Some of it has helped us survive (if you touch a hot stove, you will get burned). But a lot of it serves no real purpose and is just an artifact. He suggests that most of us wake up in the morning and think about ourselves, the things we need to do that day, and the

---

32 Dispenza, *Breaking the Habit of Being Yourself.*

problems we have to deal with. Then we anchor these thoughts in the context of our past. It's not our fault; it's how our brains work. And people don't even realize they are doing it because it is subconscious. Their brain keeps them, neurologically and chemically, within the boundaries of those past experiences. This is a severely limiting factor. It keeps us in a rut of thinking the same thoughts and making the same choices. By default, the old personality / old self is in charge.

MEDITATION AS A DEVELOPMENTAL TOOL

Meditation allows you to move from defining yourself in the context of your past to defining yourself as a vision of your future. You can imagine how powerful this can be for an athlete. Dispenza recommends a regular, scheduled morning meditation to build this future reality or change in yourself. Studies have shown that consistent meditation develops the prefrontal cortex of the brain, which is connected to higher awareness, concentration, and decision-making.[33]

> Meditation allows you to move from defining yourself in the context of your past to defining yourself as a vision of your future.

The process causes neurons to fire in new sequences and can reorganize the circuitry of the brain so that it doesn't default to serving as a filing cabinet for the past. Rather, it functions as a platform to consider the choices you are going to make and the behaviors you are going to exhibit that day and to reflect on what experiences await you. As you mentally rehearse the day, you change the chemistry of your brain. Most importantly, it

33   Adrienne A. Taren, J. David Creswell, and Peter J. Gianaros, "Dispositional Mindfulness Co-Varies with Smaller Amygdala and Caudate Volumes in Community Adults," *PLoS ONE* 8, no. 5 (2013): e64574.

can help bring you clarity about the things you are not going to do, who you are no longer going to be, and the choices you are not going to make that day. Dispenza suggests that the hardest part of change is not making the same choices we have made in the past. Daily meditation raises your awareness and puts the focus on positive change. It helps prevent us from making those negative choices on autopilot. Meditation allows us to have a clean slate in which to create anew.

Just as there was a tipping point for basketball players to engage sports psychologists, there has been a tipping point for players to consider the use of meditation. Again, it takes only a few successful people to be advocates before it becomes acceptable. Phil Jackson is probably the highest-profile early advocate of meditation. His team meditated before games to quiet their minds and to visualize success. It's hard to argue with this, as Jackson has more NBA championship rings than he has fingers to wear them. Two of the best to ever play, Kobe Bryant and Michael Jordan, worked through mindfulness practices with George Mumford, author of *The Mindful Athlete*.[34] Regular meditation became the way both players learned to deal with distractions, among other things.

I believe that teams will continually dive deeper into the mind and, someday in the not-so-distant future, unlock key components that will lead to better and better player and team development. When I was coaching with the Suns, we had a new approach to working physically with players that holistically looked at a player's body in order to help them be the best they could be. A big part of that was working with Dr. Mike Clark, a visionary who formed the National Academy of Sports Medicine and who continues to be a pioneer in that space, and Aaron Nelson, the Suns trainer at the time

---

34   George Mumford, *The Mindful Athlete: Secrets to Pure Performance* (Berkeley: Parallax Press, 2015).

who is now with the New Orleans Pelicans. Nelson is considered one of the NBA's all-time great trainers. People noticed that players like Steve Nash, Shaquille O'Neal, and Grant Hill came to the Suns at the latter part of their careers and excelled. People started to refer to Phoenix as the fountain of youth. The mind is that next frontier.

MEDITATION TESTIMONIAL

I would not recommend anything to a player that I didn't believe in or was not willing to try for myself. Meditation has been transformative for me. I had heard of meditation, but I was intrigued when I read the book *Principles*, by Ray Dalio.[35] He is the founder of Bridgewater Associates, a hedge fund that has more than $160 billion in assets under management. In his book, he credits meditation as the single most important reason for his success. He said that it helped him slow down and make better decisions during chaos. That really got my attention.

I started by meditating just three or four minutes every morning. As with physical exercise, I had to work my way up to it. I would set the timer on my phone and gradually add more time as I progressed, and I started off by focusing only on my breathing. (There are hundreds of online resources to help you get started, including many guided mediation clips on YouTube.) And as with physical exercise, I told myself that I was going to make a commitment to it. You won't see the benefits immediately. You wouldn't expect to work on increasing your vertical jump on Monday, then be disappointed if you couldn't dunk by Friday. You wouldn't expect to start a diet on Monday and expect to have lost ten pounds by the weekend. It requires practice to get it down, and it requires commitment. You

---

35   Ray Dalio, *Principles* (New York: Simon & Shuster, 2017).

have to buy into the process, and you will start to see results as you get better at it. That, for me, became very motivating.

I continue to practice mediation, and it is an important part of my daily routine. What do I gain from it? First, a sense of peace. Second, it heightens my awareness of the perspectives of other people, which in turn has helped me to be more sensitive toward others. Third, I am much more present than I ever was before. I am distracted less easily and I am tuned in to the moment in front of me rather than thinking about what happened earlier or what I have to do next. Last, I am convinced that practicing meditation has positioned me to be open to some of the great things that have happened in my life.

CHAPTER 25

DEFINE QUALITY COACHING

I don't know of any coaches who will tell you that they have never made mistakes. In fact, one of the things coaches love to do over dinner together is entertain each other with stories about the times that they really messed up. For me, I know that the many mistakes I have made in my career have only made me grow. Errors and failures, although painful when they occur, can be the biggest teachers of important lessons if you're willing to pay attention and learn from them. But I have to admit, knowing that doesn't keep me from looking back at some of my mistakes and asking myself, "What were you thinking, you knucklehead?"

EVERYTHING WAS GOING GREAT

In 2012, my agent was able to get me an interview for the head coaching job of the Portland Trailblazers. I was very prepared for the interview. I have always kept detailed notes about what I felt was important to address as a head coach. I had thoroughly studied the situation in Portland and believed that I had a deep knowledge of what I would do with that team organizationally, defensively, and offensively. In my opinion, my book was solid, and it clearly outlined what I wanted to relate to Neil O'Shea, Chad Buchanan, and the other Portland brass. I believed that I had an honest and accurate view of my strengths and weaknesses, and I knew exactly whom I would hire as assistants to round out a great staff.

I felt comfortable in the interview and thought it was going well. To illustrate the depth of my journey to becoming the best possible coach I could be, and to show my understanding of the science of personal achievement, I decided to recite my poem "A New Day." Afterward, I played it back in my head and considered it from different perspectives. At that point I said to myself, "Phil, you idiot!" I had wanted to stand out as a candidate for their coaching vacancy. From their perspective, I probably stood out, all right—as a higher-risk candidate.

I didn't get the job, but this was good. Why? Portland got a top-quality coach when they hired Terry Stotts, and I learned some critical lessons. Getting that job was not about standing out. It was about being a solid leader and teacher. It was about being a coach who players know also cares about them as people. And, most importantly, it was about being an extension of the culture that already exists with that organization.

QUALITY COACHING CHARACTERISTICS

As I mentioned, I have always paid attention to coaching effectiveness, even more so after that incident. I have had the great fortune to work with and around some of the best head coaches in basketball, and I have learned from all of them. This has allowed me to create a list of the characteristics that I think embody a great head coach, collected from the decades of my experience in the sport.

This list is not intended as a scorecard. Probably no single coach embodies every item on it. Instead, I use it as an aspirational framework. I am always striving to improve in these areas whenever I have an opportunity. What I have learned is that there are opportunities to do many of these things every single day.

Coaches wear several different hats, so I've divided this list into three categories—although there is a lot of overlap between them. First and foremost, a coach is the main voice that speaks to the team as a whole and thus sets the tone. Like any good leader, a coach must be a great communicator. In particular, they must effectively communicate a positive vision and values, the standards of integrity and performance, and an environment of trust and openness.

> Like any good leader, a coach must be a great communicator.

Positive Vision and Values

A quality coach is one who does the following:

- Has a vision that matches that of the owner and management on what the team should ultimately look like. Included in this vision are the core values that will be the lifeblood of the organization—for instance, family, sacrifice, accountability, commitment to greatness, competing with class, and belief.

- Understands that they are the main steward of those values and that catching players doing what's right is more powerful in establishing a strong culture than any type of criticism.

- Uses powerful stories about the core values playing out as a way to teach those values to all members of the organization.

- Is supremely organized. A good coach understands that they are the one who coordinates everything that goes on with the team and that they must constantly match the process to the vision.

- Believes that you can never skip steps in anything. A good coach implements a step-by-step plan in all areas of basketball operations regarding how to realize the team's vision and how to instill the core values in all personnel.

- Understands that the hiring of personnel with those values in mind is key and is done slowly and judiciously.

- Once staffing is complete, invests time in defining their roles and instilling the core values. A good coach follows that with the step-by-step implementation of how all the different departments will execute and work together.

Standards of Integrity and Performance

A quality coach is one who does the following:

- Is aware that they establish the standards that the entire team will work toward and knows that the only thing that separates levels of success are the standards that they set for the team and for themselves.

- Knows that it's not what they preach that matters but what they tolerate that will define them as a leader.

- Understands that they must always be a person of integrity and walk the talk. A good coach defines *integrity* as "when actions follow words," so they are always mindful of what they say and commit to.

- Is aware that you can never demand respect, but you command respect with who you are.

- Treats everyone the same regarding what is expected as a team member. A good coach holds everyone to the same high standard, especially themselves.

- Emphasizes a growth mentality with every person in the organization. A good coach ensures that every single day the focus is on improvement and better ways to look at things so that this growth mindset becomes a part of the team's cultural DNA.

- Focuses on asking empowering questions about how we can improve, with an emphasis on solutions instead of problems.

- Believes that the process of improvement in all people and skills depends on instilling the mindset that we will not do this until we get it right—we will do this until we know we will never get it wrong.

- Believes in tireless preparation and sets this example for the entire staff and team.

- Understands that coaching is about emphasizing. Knowing this, a good coach's practice plans are always geared toward those points of emphasis.

- Organizes their points of emphasis by using analytics that are based on efficiencies in performance.

- Pays particular attention to the early group (young players and players new to the team) who are getting in the extra work. These early sessions are always well thought out, with a plan to emphasize the needed focus.

An Environment of Trust and Openness

A quality coach is one who does the following:

- Sees themselves not simply as a coach but as a teacher.

- Looks at all members of the organization as people first. A good coach is always looking to empower as many people as possible in the organization.

- Deeply cares about all team and staff members. A good coach strives to create a true family environment, learning about all the members of their extended family.

- Knows that all players are different and that each must be coached according to their individuality to get maximum production.

- Fully believes in the vision, in the staff, and in the team. When staff and players feel that belief, they will always perform at their highest levels. The fruit of those higher levels will be a more enjoyable and productive organization that improves the assets (players) relative to their contracts. This in turn increases the potential for better trades and allows the franchise to become more valuable.

- Is low ego and teaches and delegates service leadership, in which all staff members are empowered in their work together.

- Is open minded and listens to all ideas regardless of whom they come from. A safe environment is created when staff and team members know that the goal is to simply find the best way. The fruit of this culture is when no one cares who gets the credit and all ideas are free flowing and openly shared. This allows true synergy to take place.

- Knows and completely believes in how they want to play. A good coach is aware of the best type of personnel to play that style and has mastered the step-by-step approach in order to teach that style.

- Knows that they dictate the mood and mindset of the team. A good coach wants the team's psyche to never get too high or too low, always focusing on what they can control and what comes next.

- Gains trust with the players so that they know that practices will be geared to best prepare without overdoing it. A good coach knows that you play as you practice.

CHAPTER 26

*PHI*LOSOPHY

My nature is that when I learn something, I try to teach it back. For me, an important part of that is to use phrases and quotes that get a point across in a memorable way. This goes all the way back to my first job out of college in 1985 when I worked at the University of Florida as an assistant coach for Norm Sloan. At twenty-three, I was only a couple of years older than the players. There were three guys, Jon Visscher, Eric Poms, and Bob Marinak, who had various manager roles with the team. They used to give me a hard time about the expressions and terminology I used with the players and started referring to my stuff as *Phi*losophy.

That reputation stuck with me. When I was coaching in Phoenix in 2003, we drafted Casey Jacobsen, an All-American from Stanford. He was a heck of a shooter, and he was playing well for the Suns. Because he was a rookie, I spent a lot of time working out with him.

As a result, he was on the receiving end of the variety of sayings, phrases, and adages that I use to engage and encourage players.

We called a time-out in the middle of a Suns game, and I was standing on the court in the team huddle, probably looking over Mike D'Antoni's shoulder as he talked to the players. In the NBA there is constant entertainment on the jumbotron any time there is a dead ball. During that particular time-out, they were showing prerecorded clips of question-and-answer sessions with players. Up on the screen at that moment was a close-up of Casey, and the interviewer asked, "Casey, what is your favorite quote?"

Casey didn't miss a beat. "Well, that would be from Coach Phil 'Aristotle' Weber: 'The main thing is to keep the main thing the main thing.'"

It's a funny moment that sticks out to me for two reasons. First, I'm glad Stephen Covey wasn't in the stands that night because it is his quote, not mine. But I do use it a lot because it's a great way to help players focus on their high-priority goals and not be distracted. Second, although I never intended a career as a philosopher, it is my nature to ground the things I think about in the work and studies that have already been done by great thinkers. I believe that it is a fitting way to end this book by recapping some of my favorite *Philosophies* about life, learning, and the virtuous work of getting better at something that is important to you.

LIVING IN THE PRESENT

One summer when I was coaching for the Knicks, I left the Las Vegas summer league to head back to New York. I dropped into seat 3C, stowed my gear, and selected a movie to watch. It wasn't long after that when I glanced up and to my left and noticed that the person in seat 2B was watching the same movie I was. The difference was that he had started watching the movie before me. Then I looked to my right and saw that the person in 2D had also selected the same movie, but I could tell from his screen that he had started after I did.

Every time I allowed my eyes to wander to the screen for seat 2B, I could see the future. When I looked over to 2D's screen, I could see the past. The problem was, when I did that, I would invariably have to stop my movie, rewind, and watch what I had missed.

In life we don't get to rewind. We can lose today's moments by trying to relive a time in the past under the false sense that doing so will make us feel a certain way that we're not feeling now. We can never get yesterday back, regardless of how hard we try or who we thought we were then. Time moves on, moment by moment. It doesn't matter who we were then; it won't change who we are right now. And tomorrow is not here yet, so there is no way to act on things yet to happen. All we have is this one precious moment, so we should harness our concentration on right now.

OUR MINDS CREATE OUR REALITY

What we think about grows. If we are constantly thinking about the past, then what grows? Most likely it is some nostalgic image of a time we thought was better than today. The opposite is true as well. If we are always thinking about some time in the future when we believe that things will be better, we are not improving in the present. Get control of your mind, because what you focus on is a habit. Take a moment-by-moment inventory. Where are your thoughts? Where are your energies? What does LeBron James think about today? Is it the championships he has already won, the ones he might win in the future, or the game he is playing today?

That's one of the things I really respected about Kobe Bryant. With all he accomplished, five championships and innumerable individual honors, there is not one person on this earth who gave more of his mind, body, and soul to the sport. But when interviewed right after he scored sixty points in his very last NBA game, he said very clearly that the basketball chapter of his life was finished. After that, all his focus and concentration went toward his family, his movie ideas, and his books. There is no promise of tomorrow. The only guarantee that you have is for this very moment. Treat it like the gift that it is. Be present for your family, be present for your friends, and be present for your teammates. But, most important of all, be present for yourself and fully live the life that matters for you. Because I believe that so very strongly, I suppose that means it is one of my core *Phil*osophies.

> There is no promise of tomorrow. The only guarantee that you have is for this very moment. Treat it like the gift that it is.

GUIDING PRINCIPLES

I have kept track of these beliefs, which have become my guiding principles over the years, writing them down, adding to them, and fine-tuning them as I learn more about what they mean in life. I addressed some of these throughout the book, but I have collected them here in one place for you to consider and reflect on. I hope you will find something that you can use in your own life and work as you help other people develop. Enjoy *Phil*osophy.

I believe, and believe in, the following:

- *Family, love, and support.* To me, the purpose of life is being able to share success and failure and to be there so that others can do the same.

- *Ordinary people do extraordinary things every day.* With a growth mindset, determination, and focus, everybody is capable of doing amazing things.

- *People are inherently good.* That's the lens through which I choose to look at the world. I tend to trust people more than not. Abraham Lincoln said that he would rather go through life trusting people and getting let down every once in a while than go through life not trusting anyone and being miserable.

- *Giving.* I believe that if you give to others without expectation of return, magic happens. I think that giving is what this world should be about—giving of ourselves to help others. Because when you do, everyone benefits.

- *Empowering habits.* Our language can be disempowering or empowering. We should monitor not only our language but also our thoughts. Thoughts create habits, and those habits can either propel us to improve or to go backward.

- *Exercise benefits the mind and the body.* When I exercise, my body releases a pharmacy of positive chemicals into my body. Exercise gives me more energy, better peace of mind, and a sense of accomplishment.

- *Gratitude.* I believe that it changes us. If you mindfully count your blessings every single day and acknowledge how fortunate you are and how precious this day is, it changes your view of the world.

- *Every day is a gift.* This is what we have. We don't have any guarantee of tomorrow. Being here today is a gift. That's why it is called the *present.*

- *Not everybody should get a trophy.* In the interest of making everyone feel good, we reward them all, and life isn't like that. I've grown so much more from working through my setbacks and defeats than I ever have from my successes. There is a great book about this by Ryan Holiday titled *The Obstacle Is the Way.*[36]

- *There are no justified resentments … ever.* When we allow the things that we think other people have done to us to dominate our minds, it is like a poison circulating inside us. Forgive people, and the poison goes away. This takes work.

- *Service leadership.* This means that we must see ourselves as servants to others before we see ourselves as leaders. Servant leadership is all about serving others by providing direction that allows them to grow.

- *By continuing to improve ourselves, we positively impact the world.* In his book *Power vs. Force*, David Hawkins states that self-improvement not only has a positive impact but also counterbalances some of the negativity in the world by our level of consciousness.[37] The baseline for positive is 200. Gandhi calibrated at 490 and, without weapons, was able to influence his country's freedom.

- *Our minds are the next frontier.* Our brain is so complex, and we're only beginning to understand the amazing things that

---

36 Ryan Holiday, *The Obstacle Is the Way: The Timeless Art of Turning Trials into Triumph* (New York: Penguin Group, 2014).

37 David R. Hawkins, *Power vs. Force* (Carlsbad, CA: Hay House, 2014).

it can do. In basketball and in life, the next performance breakthrough will be all about the mind.

- *We should treat people as we believe they can be.* This is a powerful concept in teaching and coaching. If you believe in and can picture that person performing at their best possible level, you teach or coach them differently, even if you don't realize it.

- *Complete forgiveness.* Holding a grudge is giving your power away. Championship boxer Rubin "Hurricane" Carter did not hold anger in his heart for the people who falsely convicted him of murder at the height of his career. When he was finally freed from prison, he simply went about his life. He said that if he had held on to the anger, he would say to the world that they took something from him, and he refused to allow that.

- *The only way we rid ourselves of a bad habit is by instilling a new and better one.* You have to analyze and be a student of the habits you have. By doing so, you can make significant change in your life. This is one of the many *Phi*losophies that I derived from Og Mandino's book *The Greatest Salesman in the World.*[38]

- *When you learn something, you should teach it.* Doing so gives you a deeper understanding. It also makes you accountable to what you just taught someone else. It holds you to a higher standard.

- *How you do anything is how you do everything.* Winning is a habit, as is doing your best.

---

38 Mandino, *The Greatest Salesman in the World.*

- *We teach others how to treat us.* And we do it by how we treat them. If you are patient with others, they'll be patient with you. If you are trusting with others, they will be trusting toward you. It's very powerful.

- *What a person can conceive of and believe, they can achieve.* This is from Napoleon Hill's book *Think and Grow Rich*. It's our beliefs that guide us. If you turn those beliefs into convictions, you won't be able to shake them. This can drive positive change in your life.

- *There is a space between action and reaction.* This is from Holocaust survivor Viktor Frankel, whose point was that in that space, we have the power to choose how we respond and the type of person we want to be. Are you reactionary, or when something happens to you, do you align yourself with the type of person you want to be?

- *Our language is like a fingerprint.* It tells the world who we are. It shows a growth versus a fixed mindset by the words we use. We have to be purposeful about our word choices because words have energy. Choose to be empowered.

- *What we think about grows.* We are constantly thinking, and a lot of our thoughts are habitual. If we think about problems, they grow. But if our mind is attuned to solutions, they grow. Look for the solution. Don't dwell on problems.

- *The quality of our life boils down to the quality of the questions we continue to ask ourselves.* Two different people could face identical bad situations, with one person asking, "Why did that have to happen to me?" The other person asks, "How can I grow from this?" or "How can I help someone else as a result of this?" The first question disempowers and sets in motion more negativity; the second and third empower and direct you toward solutions.

- *The ego cannot live in the moment.* It's either in the past or in the future. This is another reason to live in the present. When we begin to compare people, it's usually about ego.

- *We should never argue for our limitations.* Writer Richard Bach stated that if you argue for your limitations, you get to keep them. When people put energy into defending, explaining, or justifying their limitations, they lose. This happens most often when someone else suggests that there are ways to overcome the things that challenge us. Again, be mindful of your language.

- *Mental toughness is developed.* Don't shy away from hard work and tough situations. Embrace the struggle and you will grow.

- *It's not what happens to us that matters.* What matters is our interpretation. If we are always aligned with our empowered beliefs, our interpretations will empower us.

- *Self-discipline is self-love.* Do we do things for immediate gratification (that will later cause us to shake our heads with guilt), or do we forgo immediate gratification and develop more intralove?

- *How you make people feel makes the real difference.* As the poet Maya Angelou said, "People will forget what you said, people will forget what you did, but people will never forget how you made them feel."[39]

---

39   Barbara Quirk, "Women Need to Feel Good about Themselves," *Capital Times,*

- *Push forward with no regrets.* The mistakes and hardships we've experienced were supposed to happen because they strengthen us for what's ahead.

- *This too shall pass.* Good or bad, it always does. These are four magic words that get us through all things.

- *Judgment and understanding are opposite sides of the same coin.* If you judge, you have not taken the time to understand, and if you fully understand, you will never judge. In today's divisive world, we need more empathy and real caring for others.

These are all principles that I try to apply to my work with players and with others in my life. I'm not perfect about living up to them, but each day I am motivated to be better at them than I was the day before. Although they have all been useful to me over the course of my career, I have saved for last the one that is, in my mind, the most significant. It's not necessarily more important than the others, but I believe that it is the most comprehensive. From my experience, it underpins everything that we do as humans.

- *Life is made up of levels.* If you're climbing a mountain, the view at the bottom isn't very good. When you put in some effort, the view improves, but it's not great. As you continue to move up the levels, the view improves gradually and then substantially when you make it to the top. You're tired, but the view is so worth it. Everything in our lives has levels. Relationships have levels, mastery has levels, and knowledge has levels. Self-awareness has levels. Marriage has levels. What are the important mountains in your life? Understand that there

---

July 22, 2003, 4D.

are always different levels. The easy way out, and the path of least resistance, is to always stay near the bottom. Or, just as bad, to go up one level and try to convince yourself that you are done because you are better off than you used to be. Don't settle. Just think what the view is like from the top.

This book is about helping others develop, whether it is a basketball player, a student, a coworker, or a child. As you have gleaned from reading it, I believe that a large part of that process involves developing ourselves as well. We have to deploy the same growth mindset that we expect from those with whom we work.

THE STORY OF THE GOLDEN BUDDHA

In Thailand there is a ten-foot-tall statue of Buddha made out of gold. No one knows what year it was built, but scholars estimate sometime between the thirteenth and fourteenth centuries. At some point, to keep it from being stolen, the monks covered the golden Buddha with a layer of concrete made with sparkling glass. Over the course of its lifetime, even though it had been moved several times, it remained covered in that concrete casing. The monks who knew that there was gold under the plaster all eventually died. Then, in 1955, while being moved again, it was accidentally dropped, and a chunk of concrete fell off to reveal the gold hidden beneath. Historians carefully removed the rest of the plaster to reveal the beautiful Buddha that had lived for centuries under the rough outer layer.

Why did I save this story for the end of the book? I believe that because of the way we're raised, socialized, or educated, we are all covered with layers of clay, limiting belief on top of limiting belief. To me, those layers of clay are a symbol of every limiting belief that has been placed on us. I'm convinced that the most important thing

I ever did for any basketball player was to believe in them, even when they didn't have the same belief in themselves. I believe that there is gold under the plaster in everyone I meet. My quest has been to try to work with players to remove the concrete to reveal the golden potential inside each and every one of them. That is the cornerstone of the work we do to help people become the best they can be, and everything else builds off it.

Now, go make them thirsty!

ACKNOWLEDGMENTS

When I was born I hit the lottery, not from a financial perspective but from a family perspective. My mom and dad instilled in me and my two sisters, Laurie and Sharon, the value of family, hard work, humility, and love. To this day, I don't think my dad or mom have ever "slept in." My dad was a full-time teacher and coach but never wanted our family to want for anything, so he started a business cleaning shopping centers while still teaching and coaching a full day. My mom was a full-time mom, the bookkeeper and overall family chauffeur and problem solver. We kids never missed a practice, game, or school event. Never. The love and support my whole family has shown me could never be surpassed.

I have been so blessed by all the coaches and teachers who have helped me all along the way as a player and as a coach and who allowed me into their practices and shared with me knowledge and experiences. I want to thank them all—some have left us for a better place.

The Rev: RIP; so much of what you instilled in me my high school days I still and will always use with players I work with. Coach Sloan: RIP; thanks for seeing something in me and my scholarship as a player, and also for my very first job as a coach. V: thanks for inspiring me and for instilling in me a curiosity to understand everything about self-esteem. Coach Wooden: RIP; having had only a one-time meeting and then a pen pal relationship showed a vision of such a quality individual, learned and caring, basically a vision of all the qualities in a person I have attempted to live up to since. Darryl Lauderdale: thanks for giving me the opportunity to get back into coaching at Chaminade University in Hawaii. Jerry Welsh: thanks for the opportunity to work with another tremendous person and teacher at Iona College. Bret Bearup: RIP; thanks to one of my lifetime friends for hiring me and, unbeknownst to either one of us, setting me on a path to fulfill my passion; you were one of the smartest and funniest people this world has ever known. I miss you daily.

Thanks to all the players who have let me work with them, allowing me to grow in so many ways as a coach and a person. Without your focus, hard work, belief in yourself, and extreme dedication, this book would not be possible. Thanks to the agents Jeff Schwartz, Bill Duffy, Thaddeus Foucher, Andy Miller, Arn Tellem, and Dan Fegan (RIP), who allowed me to work with their players and draft guys. Thanks to Danny Ainge, an amazing person, player, coach, and now executive director of the Boston Celtics, for seeing the future of where the NBA was going and changing not only my life but my family's life with the opportunity of a lifetime. Thanks to Jerry Colangelo for allowing an out-of-coaching coach to jump to the bench of the NBA and also illustrating in all your actions what integrity really looks like. Thanks to Bryan Colangelo: as father like son, you have been so instrumental in my career in so many ways, and I deeply value your friendship and advice.

Thanks to all the coaches who have hired me in the NBA: Scott Skiles, Frank Johnson, Mike D'Antoni, Erik Spoelstra, and Alvin Gentry. Your friendship and belief in me has enhanced my life in so many ways.

A special thanks to Mike D'Antoni, who actually had to put up with my pestering him with my offense ideas for ten years, and to Erik Spoelstra, who invited me in during one of the most intense times in his life—we would sometimes disagree like brothers, but the deepest respect is always there, and our "war rooms" would make a great movie someday.

Thanks to all my front office friends, from whom I have learned so much about our league—there are so many of you.

A special thank-you to the Miami Heat, Coach Riley, Andy Elisburg, and my GM Adam Simon for giving me my first opportunity to be a head coach.

To all the people who have fired me or didn't hire me, who are countless: thank you for the gift of adversity, because it has been in those times that I have truly grown the most.

Thanks to all my close friends and advisors: Danny Ferry, Roger Maris Jr., Dennis Kelly, Jim Caviezel, Greg Ruggles, Peter Borish, Richard Thompson, Bryan Reynolds, Jon Visscher, Terry Gannon, Thurl Bailey, Sidney Lowe, Howie Frankel, Kent Katich, Tim Thoreson, Jeff Feinberg, Steve Stowe, Todd Brooke, Andy Starr, Roger Dreyer, Danielle Cantor, Mike Clark, all my NC State crew, the Gator Boys, and so many I have not mentioned. Friendship and sharing experiences are what make life truly worth living.

Thanks to all the growth-mindset crew of my NBA world: Noel Gillespie, Rich Fernando, Alex Klein, Matt Whinrey, Somak Sakar,

Matt Riccardi, Jason Brown, Harley Borish, and my nephew Steven Klei; your futures are bright due to your work ethic, mindset, and the way you greet each day.

And last, I want to thank the stars of my life. My amazing wife, Lila, who has supported and believed in me every step of my journey, and the newest star, my daughter Soleil, who stole my heart the second I laid eyes on her. You guys are my inspiration.

Phil Weber is an expert on the subject of player and personal development. In college Phil was a point guard on Jim Valvano's Cardiac Pack at North Carolina State University. After college Phil landed coaching positions at the University of Florida, Chaminade University, and Iona University. But it is in the NBA that Phil has had the most impact by combining his basketball knowledge and philosophical approach to the physical and mental development of basketball players. He has coached the bench for the Phoenix Suns and the New York Knicks, was offensive consultant for the world champion Miami Heat, was head coach for the Heat's G League team, the Skyforce, and coached for the New York Pelicans before moving to their front office. A philosopher at heart, Phil lives the values he teaches, always reading, always writing, and always learning.

A visit with Coach Wooden at his home, a day that profoundly
changed the way I looked at coaching and life

A great night in Denver, meeting up with my Knicks rookie Gallo,
his brother Federico, and my good friend Bear

A special night for Boris Diaw, accepting the
Most Improved Player Award

A special night with Erik Spoelstra and our very close
mutual friend and Heat VP Steve Stowe, presenting me
with my 2013 NBA Championship ring

At the Coliseum in Rome: basketball has enriched my life
in so many ways, allowing me to see the world and
meet so many incredible people.

Before a game in Denver with Bear, my lifelong friend who
unknowingly changed the trajectory of my life

Coaching a game in the NBA Summer League: such a tremendous
opportunity to work on Xs and Os

My first press conference as a head coach,
an opportunity I'm so grateful for

With one of my all-time favorite rookies, Leandro Barbosa

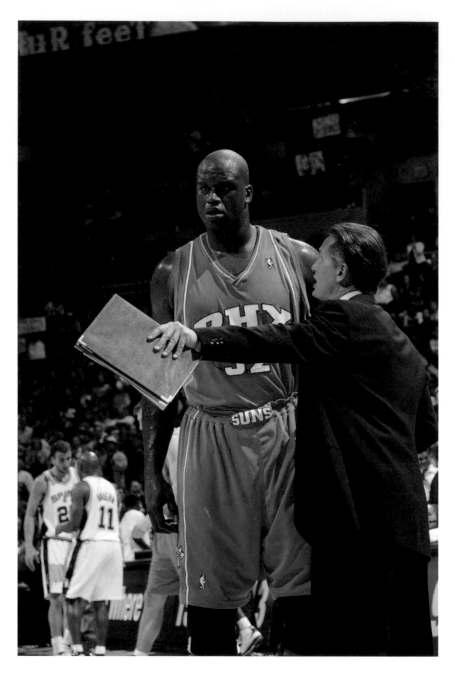

I was humbled and honored to be able to work with Shaq, arguably the most dominant player the NBA has ever seen.

Leandro Barbosa accepting the well-deserved
NBA Sixth Man Award

My first practice as a head coach, with my goal to hopefully come close to instilling the amazing Heat culture

Shawn, Amar'e, and Steve at the 2005 All-Star Game: great players, but better people

Our Phoenix coaching staff representing the West in the All-Star
Game in Las Vegas

Western Conference Finals against the Spurs: Amar'e, Shawn, Q,
and JJ (with his fractured orbital bone); missing from this picture is
Steve, who made this machine roll.

My first playoff game as a head coach with Sioux Falls:
we won our division and faced off against Canton.

Working with Mike D'Antoni was so much fun; winning was also always extremely enjoyable!

With Toney Douglas, a super hard worker: Summer League is for growth, as a coach and as a player.